CANCER ANSWERS

CANCER ANSWERS

Encouraging Answers to 25 Questions
You Were Always Afraid to Ask

Errol C. Friedberg, M.D.

W. H. FREEMAN AND COMPANY
NEW YORK

Library of Congress Cataloging-in-Publication Data

Friedberg, Errol C.
    Cancer answers: encouraging answers to 25 questions you were always
afraid to ask / Errol C. Friedberg
        p.   cm.
    Includes index.
    ISBN 0-7167-7023-7
    1. Cancer—Popular works.   2. Cancer—Miscellanea.   I. Title.
RC263.F74   1992
616.99'4—dc20   92-13491
                                                                    CIP

Printed in the United States of America

1 2 3 4 5 6 7 8 9 0 VB 9 9 8 7 6 5 4 3 2

*This book is dedicated
to the cancer patients of the world
and to their families.*

CONTENTS

Preface   xiii

To the Reader   xv

QUESTION 1
What is cancer?   1

QUESTION 2
Why does the uncontrolled growth   7
of cells cause illness and death?

QUESTION 3
What are the early symptoms   11
of cancer?

QUESTION 4
What's the difference between   21
a cancer and a tumor?

QUESTION 5
What's the difference between   25
benign and malignant tumors?

QUESTION 6
Can benign tumors become   27
malignant?

QUESTION 7
What's the difference between   31
carcinoma, sarcoma, leukemia,
and lymphoma?

Contents

QUESTION 8
How is cancer diagnosed?   37

QUESTION 9
What are my chances of developing   43
cancer and dying from it?

QUESTION 10
Why is cancer so common?   49

QUESTION 11
What causes cells to become   59
cancerous?

QUESTION 12
How do agents that cause cancer do   65
their dirty work?

QUESTION 13
How quickly does a cancer grow?   73

QUESTION 14
Can I catch cancer from someone?   81

QUESTION 15
Do I have natural defenses against   85
cancer?

QUESTION 16
Can one be born with an increased   93
risk of getting cancer?

QUESTION 17
How can I reduce my risk   99
of cancer?

Contents

QUESTION 18
How do cancer treatments
work?   111

QUESTION 19
Who can help me make   121
decisions about cancer treatment?

QUESTION 20
What about alternative cancer   133
treatments?

QUESTION 21
What are my chances of   139
surviving cancer?

QUESTION 22
Why don't treatments for   147
cancer always result in a cure?

QUESTION 23
What's the future of cancer   151
treatment?

QUESTION 24
Is there a connection between   157
cancer and one's emotional state?

QUESTION 25
How do I get more information   163
about cancer?

Index   185

*There is not enough darkness in all the world to put
out the light of even one small candle.*

Robert Alden

*Light breaks where no sun shines:
Where no sea runs, the waters of the heart
Push in their tides.*

Dylan Thomas

Preface

The knowledge that we have or might have cancer strikes a terrifying chord in most of us. Indeed, a former senior official in a government health regulatory agency once stated insightfully that "cancer has come to have a special place in our perception of illness; it is the disease Americans fear more than they fear war." One out of every five people in the United States and many other countries in the world is expected to die of cancer. Aside from the physical complications of the disease, its frequency and its typically lingering course extract a harsh emotional toll on patients and loved ones alike.

For many years I have observed that people who are diagnosed with cancer face a distressing informational vacuum about many aspects of the disease: what it is, how common it is, how it happens, how it is diagnosed and treated, what the chances of survival are, and what medical and scientific communities are doing about it. This book attempts to address that vacuum. It is intended primarily for people who have an interest in learning the facts about cancer, but who have neither the time nor the energy to absorb complicated biological concepts and bewildering medical terminology. Because this book is neither a textbook nor a technical discussion of cancer, it requires little or no formal background in biology and presumes no particular information about cancer. It can be easily read in an evening or two.

It is of course impossible to talk about cancer without using some technical terms. I have tried to keep these to a minimum and to explain them as simply as possible. A glossary of all the technical terms used in the text is included at the end of the book.

If you have or have had cancer, or know and care about someone who does, it is my hope that this book will provide you with a firm initial framework for more detailed readings on the topic and for understanding your discussions with health professionals. Above all, I hope that this book will offer you a new sense of optimism about the great strides that have been made in understanding and treating cancer and will stimulate you to learn more about this extremely important health problem.

I wish to acknowledge the many students and professional colleagues who over the years have sharpened my interest in and curiosity about the field of cancer and who have challenged my ability to communicate and teach the subject of cancer biology effectively. Particular thanks are due to Jane Cooper for her insightful feedback on numerous drafts of the text. I am indebted to my wife, Anne Bowcock, and to my parents-in-law, Pauline and John Bowcock, for their interest from the very inception of this project and for many helpful comments and suggestions. Thanks are also due to Lee Bardwell and Rob McKenna for their careful review of the manuscript and to Mary Thurston for her conscientious logistical support and invaluable help with reference materials. I also wish to acknowledge *Ca—A Cancer Journal for Clinicians,* published by the American Cancer Society, for providing all the relevant statistical information in this book. Finally, I wish to acknowledge Natalie Bowen for her insightful and skilled editing, and, at W. H. Freeman, Ingrid Krohn, Senior Editor, for her immediate understanding of what I wanted to achieve, Linda Chaput, President, for her enthusiastic support of this project, and the other members of the Freeman staff who helped bring the work to fruition.

Errol C. Friedberg, M.D.

To the Reader:

Whether you are a cancer patient, or a relative or friend of someone who is, it is my hope that this book does indeed answer many of the fundamental questions that surface for you about this disease. As the author of the book, a practicing scientist and physician, and an educator, I invite your comments and suggestions so that the future editions of CANCER ANSWERS can be as helpful, and hopeful, as possible.

Errol C. Friedberg, M.D.

Please send your comments to me at:

Department of Pathology
The University of Texas Southwestern Medical Center at Dallas
Dallas, Texas 75235-9072

What is cancer?

1

*All interest in disease and death
is only another expression
of interest in life.*
　　　　　　　—Thomas Mann

Cancer is a process during which cells in the body grow in an uncontrolled fashion. The word comes from the Latin for "crab," and both the disease and the zodiacal sign *Cancer* acquired their names because of their crablike appearance. Many years ago when surgeons first began to remove cancers from people, they were struck by the fact that when they cut them open to examine them the cancers often had a pattern that looked something like a crab. Later in the book we'll talk more about exactly why the growth of cancer cells produces this crablike appearance. But other than this curious coincidence of pattern formation in the eyes of early observers of stars and of human tissues, the disease has nothing to do with astrology (as far as we know!).

What exactly do we mean by the *uncontrolled growth of cells?* Perhaps the simplest way to understand this is to understand how the uncontrolled growth of cells differs from their controlled growth. But before we explore this concept any further let's be sure we clearly understand what cells are.

Cells are the fundamental units of all living things. The word comes from the Latin *cella*, meaning "compartment," which is really an excellent description, because cells are indeed tiny compartments or units of life. Every organ and tissue in the body is composed of cells, all of which are basically alike, but differ somewhat in their functions according to the organ they belong to.

Cells are very tiny. A typical living cell is only about one five-hundred thousandth of an inch long, far too small to see with the naked eye. So it requires a microscope to be able to see cells. The average adult person consists of about three trillion (three million million) cells. To give you some idea of just how large a number this is, if we laid out all the cells of the body end to end we would have about 375 miles of cells.

When we talk about growth we usually think about something getting bigger, as in the growth of a child or a tree. But during the growth of a child, or a puppy, or a tree, individual cells do not get bigger, they increase in number. So when we talk about cell growth we really mean *an increase in the number of cells.*

Cells increase in number by a process whereby one cell (called the parent cell) divides and gives rise to two cells (called daughter cells). These two cells in turn become parents and each gives rise to two new daughters so that we now have four cells, and so on. This process is called *cell division.* (Don't get confused by the fact that cells multiply by division!) During cell division all of the components of the cell are duplicated so that when the cell divides—splits in two—each new cell gets every component that its parent had and so the two cells are identical.

Let's consider some familiar examples of controlled or regulated growth of cells. One of the most fascinating is the process by which a single fertilized human ovum, or egg, gives rise to a newborn baby over a period of about nine months. In a similar vein, did you ever keep a chicken's egg in a warm place until after a matter of only weeks a fully developed chick, complete with chirp, emerged?

These amazing processes involve the expansion of one single cell into many billions of cells. Although it may not be immediately obvious, if one cell divides into two daughter cells and each of them divides again to give rise to four cells, and so on, the number of cells can reach an extremely large number (such as three trillion) rather rapidly. Let me demonstrate this by asking the following question:

Would you give me a job for just a single month at a starting wage of one penny a day, doubling my salary every day? Most people's immediate intuition is to answer in the affirmative. After all, one penny is absolute peanuts as a starting wage. And even if you doubled this every day how much can it really come to in just thirty days? Well, if you examine the numbers in the following table you might be shocked at the size of the financial commitment you would be making. On day 1 you would pay me one cent, but by day 30 you would have to pay me $5,368,709.12! This rapid increase in size is called exponential growth.

At the same time as the actual number or mass of cells expands during the formation of babies and chickens (and, for that matter, plants and trees), these billions of cells also change and become organized into different organs and tissues such as a heart and lungs and a brain and eyes and bones and muscles. So cells not only increase in number, but during normal growth they change into different types and also assume particular assigned positions in different parts of the body. Clearly some extraordinarily precise and complicated biological programs must be unfolding for all of this to happen so perfectly and so reproducibly.

Such programs are what we mean by the *controlled* growth of cells, in which every cell in an animal or plant—a living thing or organism—behaves exactly the way it is supposed to for the entire life of that organism. We don't have to concern ourselves with the details of how the programs that determine controlled growth actually work. In fact, at the present time we understand very little about this complicated process.

The controlled growth of cells does not stop at birth. Childhood and adolescence are also accompanied by an orderly increase of cells in different tissues and organs. For instance, during childhood baby teeth are replaced by a permanent set of teeth, and bones expand. Young women develop breasts at the time of puberty, and young men sprout hair on their faces. The controlled growth of cells

The Phenomenon of Exponential Growth

Day	Payment by You	Day	Payment by You
1	1 cent	16	$327.68
2	2 cents	17	$655.36
3	4 cents	18	$1,310.72
4	8 cents	19	$2,621.44
5	16 cents	20	$5,242.88
6	32 cents	21	$10,485.76
7	64 cents	22	$20,971.52
8	$1.28	23	$41,943.04
9	$2.56	24	$83,886.08
10	$5.12	25	$167,772.16
11	$10.24	26	$335,544.32
12	$20.48	27	$671,088.64
13	$40.96	28	$1,342,177.28
14	$81.92	29	$2,684,354.56
15	$163.84	30	$5,368,709.12

also goes on in adult organisms. Think for a moment about the fact that every year mature fruit trees burst forth with hundreds of new fruits, each of which which starts as a tiny blossom.

In the human body, loss and renewal of cells is a constant process. In an adult person consisting of about three trillion cells, an estimated 350 billion of them divide every day. Why does this happen? Well, each day you shed millions of cells from your skin, from the lining of your intestines, the lining of your airway, and from various other parts of your body. During the process of menstruation millions of cells are shed from the lining of the womb each month and a new lining of cells forms. Whenever you scratch your skin you displace thousands of cells. Every time you sneeze you shed cells from your sinuses and nose, and every time you cough you shed cells from your lungs and your mouth. All of these lost cells must be replaced by new ones, which arise by the regulated (controlled) growth of their parent cells.

Despite the fact that all of these processes involving the growth of cells are so highly regulated and controlled, they are not absolutely perfect and every now and again something does go wrong. For example, during the growth of a tiny embryo into a baby, the growth program sometimes gets scrambled and an arm or a leg or the heart or some other organ doesn't form properly. We call such examples of abnormal growth *congenital defects* or *congenital malformations*.

In addition to these particular growth problems that occur before birth and which result in congenital defects, any time after a normal infant is born some aspect of the complicated programs that control the growth of cells can go wrong and *cells in the body can begin to grow when they shouldn't*. When this type of uncontrolled growth occurs the result is cancer. This, then, is what we mean when we talk about cancer as the *uncontrolled* growth of cells.

Why does the uncontrolled growthof cells cause illness and death?

2

Visualize in your mind's eye a single cancer cell somewhere in the body—a cell that is no longer a member of the team, so to speak, and that begins to multiply at a time when it should not. Imagine also that this process of untimely cell division by this "rebel" cancer cell continues to the point that we now have a tiny collection of cells, perhaps only a few hundred in number. At this stage in the history of a cancer, when it consists of just a few hundred or even a few thousand cells, we have no way of detecting it because it is too small. Remember that a single cell is only about one five hundred thousandth of an inch long. If a cancer consisting of one thousand cells somewhere in the body is shaped like a cube, each side of the cube would be much smaller than the head of a pin. So people with such a tiny cancer are totally unaware of its presence in their bodies. They feel in perfect health because at this stage the tiny cancer usually causes no ill effects whatsoever.

But as the cancer cells continue to multiply, ignoring the controls that regulate the growth of normal cells, the cancer gets progressively bigger until it begins to make its presence felt in some way; that is, it produces symptoms. How soon this happens and exactly what type of symptoms will depend very much on where the cancer is growing. If it is growing near the surface of the body, for example, in a breast or testicle, or in a muscle or bone just under the skin, or in any other part of the body that is easily accessible by feel, it may be discovered accidentally during the course of some routine daily activity. One might, for example, be idly scratching oneself or washing in the shower and discover a lump or a bump where there shouldn't be one. These chance discoveries frequently take place without any evidence of discomfort, pain, or any other noticeable symptoms. You should be aware that not every such lump or bump is necessarily cancer and we will consider in Question 4 the difference between those that are and those that are not. But for the moment let's pursue the immediate question at hand: How does this mass of growing cells cause disease and, if untreated, eventually death?

At the same time that a cancer is increasing in size because of an increase in the number of cells, individual cancer cells begin to show other forms of deviant behavior that we never observe in normal cells. Normal cells always respect the territory of their neighbors. For example, the cells in your skin are arranged in multiple layers. In each layer the cells form a perfectly organized pattern, much like the stones in a mosaic, or the pieces in a jigsaw puzzle. Cells in any one layer don't pile up on top of one another. And cells that belong in one layer never move up or down to the next layer.

Cancer cells don't respect these territorial boundaries. They invade their immediate surroundings, literally shoving normal neighboring cells out of the way. The result is that at the same time a cancer increases in size it also spreads out in all directions. This process of spreading into the surrounding tissue is called *invasion*, a very apt word because cancer cells do indeed infiltrate the surrounding tissues just like an invading army. No tissues of the body are protected from this invasive process. Even tissue as hard as bone can be invaded by cancer cells.

By the time a cancer is big enough to actually be felt as a lump or a bump, it consists of many millions of cells. If such a lump were surgically removed from the body and cut open, what would it look like? As I mentioned earlier, in the very early days of medicine physicians were rather imaginative in their descriptions of diseased organs and tissues and often made comparisons to familiar objects in the physical world. If we stretch our imaginations, as did the physicians who described the appearance of cancers hundreds of years ago, we might indeed agree that many cancers do sort of resemble a crab. This resemblance derives from the process of *invasion* resulting in numerous "clawlike" extensions which radiate in all directions from a central "body."

You can readily imagine that as a cancer increases in size and invades the surrounding tissues it will begin to interfere with the normal functioning of that tissue. Let's consider a cancer growing somewhere in the brain. As normal brain cells are shoved out of the way or become surrounded and separated from their neighbors by the aggressively growing cancer cells, they are unable to function properly, and frequently die. Obviously, when normal cells lose their function so does the organ to which they belong. So a person with brain cancer will eventually develop symptoms indicative of abnormal brain function. These will vary depending on which particular part of the brain is affected. Similarly, if a cancer is growing in a lung one may experience difficulty in breathing, or may develop a persistent cough or some other respiratory symptom.

What are the early symptoms of cancer?

3

Our safety is not in blindness,
but in facing our danger.
—Johann Cristoph Schiller

Regrettably, in many instances cancers do not produce symptoms
until the disease is quite advanced. However, many of the more common types of cancer are often associated with symptoms that are
referable to the particular organ or part of the body affected. These
early symptoms can be quite subtle and therefore there is a common
tendency to ignore them, especially if they are periodic in nature
and not associated with pain or disability. But it is precisely for this
reason that one should pay attention to them and consult professional help as soon as possible. Here are some of the most frequently
encountered symptoms that arise from the common types of cancer.
In perusing this list keep in mind that all of these symptoms can be
caused by myriad other diseases that have nothing to do with cancer.
The important "red flag" is their persistence over many weeks or
months, and the tendency for the symptoms to get worse.

General Symptoms Caused by Many Different Types of Cancer

Persistent tiredness for no obvious reason.

Progressive loss of weight for no obvious reason.

Progressive paleness of the tongue or fingernail beds, especially
if accompanied by fatigue. Paleness and fatigue can mean that
one is slowly losing blood and hence becoming anemic.

Persistent loss of appetite.

Fracture of a bone without any obvious trauma. This can be caused by spread of a cancer from any place in the body to a bone.

Cancer of the Colon and Rectum

Persistent diarrhea or constipation.

Blood in the stool. The blood can be either bright red in color or dark brown, or even black if the blood has aged.

Stools that are much narrower than normal.

Loss of weight for no apparent reason.

A feeling that one has not emptied one's bowel completely.

General discomfort in the stomach area, such as bloating, fullness or cramps, or gas pains.

Cancer of the Breast

A lump or bump or even a feeling of thickening in the breast or in the armpit.

A change in the texture of the nipple or the pink tissue (often brown in women who have had children) called the *areola,* which immediately surrounds the nipple.

Any discharge from the nipple.

Any change in the shape of one breast.

Cancer of the Lung

A persistent cough not associated with a cold or the flu.

Persistent chest pain, which may or may not be related to coughing.

Persistent hoarseness.

Coughing up blood.

Shortness of breath for no apparent reason.

Frequent and persistent respiratory infections, such as bronchitis or even pneumonia.

Cancer of the Stomach

Any persistent and unexplained abdominal pain or discomfort, including indigestion or heartburn.

Vomiting, especially vomiting blood.

Cancer of the Cervix or Uterus

Bleeding between normal menstrual periods.

Bleeding after intercourse or after a pelvic examination.

A persistent discharge from the vagina.

Cancer of the Pancreas

Cancer of the pancreas is particularly problematic because it frequently does not produce early symptoms. For this reason it is often referred to as "silent" cancer. One should pay particular attention to:

Persistent pain in the abdomen, particularly if it spreads to the back.

A yellow discoloration of the skin and the whites of the eyes, called *jaundice*. This can be caused by cancer of the pancreas blocking the duct (tube) through which bile normally flows.

Persistent loss of appetite.

Persistent nausea.

Cancer of the Lymph Glands (Lymphoma)

Lymphoma is a cancer that affects the lymph glands in the body and is discussed in greater detail later in the book. The important early symptoms of lymphoma include the following:

Painless swelling of the lymph glands in the neck, armpits, or groin.

Heavy sweating during the night.

Persistent itching of the skin for no apparent reason.

The development of red patches on the skin.

Persistent and unexplained nausea and vomiting.

Leukemia in Adults

Enlarged lymph glands as described above for lymphoma.

Persistent bone pain.

A tendency to bleed or bruise easily.

A sense of heaviness or fullness under the left ribs, due to enlargement of the spleen.

Frequent infections anywhere in the body.

Melanoma of the Skin (also see Question 6)

Any change in the size, shape, or color of a mole.

A tendency for a mole that one has had for a long time to bleed or to ooze, or to become tender, painful, or itchy.

The appearance of a new mole.

Cancer of the Bladder

Any bleeding with urination, with or without pain.

Cancer of the Testicles

A lump in either of the testicles.

Persistent pain or discomfort in the testicles.

A sudden collection of fluid in the scrotum—the bag of skin in which the testicles lie.

Any enlargement or swelling of either testicle.

Persistent pain or even a dull ache in the groin or lower abdomen.

Enlargement or tenderness of the breasts. This can result from hormonal imbalances caused by certain cancers of the testicle.

Remember that none of the symptoms described above necessarily mean that one has cancer. In fact, all of them can be caused by many different diseases, many of which are quite innocuous. But consulting a doctor if any of these symptoms is persistent is the smartest way of eliminating the worrying possibility of cancer, and is the most effective way of diagnosing and treating the disease early.

The relationship between the time of onset of symptoms and the size of a cancer is very variable and really depends very much on which organ is affected and exactly where in that organ the cancer is growing. A cancer in a vital organ such as the brain may be the size of a pea when it begins to interfere with brain functions. On the other hand cancer of the intestine may be much larger before one is aware of any disturbance in health. The reason for this is the length of the intestines (over twenty feet), so that the destruction of a small part of the intestine by cancer cells usually doesn't noticeably interfere with overall intestinal function. Other examples of which this is true are breast cancer and skin cancer. The presence of a progressively enlarging cancer in the breast or the skin really doesn't impair one's health because it doesn't affect any function that is absolutely needed for good health.

But unfortunately cancers don't only grow at and infiltrate into the immediate site where the problem started. They also spread to other parts of the body—becoming just as large and invading just as extensively as at the original site. So the problem with cancer of the intestine or cancer of the breast or cancer of the skin is not so much the effect that an expanding mass of cancer cells has on those particular organs, but—much more importantly—the fact that cancer cells spread to other parts of the body, so that life-sustaining organs such as the brain, lungs, liver, heart, and kidneys eventually become compromised and are no longer able to function properly.

This phenomenon of spread to other parts of the body constitutes the single most important problem in the diagnosis and the effective treatment of cancer. If cancers could always be detected before they had spread to other parts of the body they could probably be cured in most, if not all, cases. But for reasons that will later become clear, it is extremely difficult to eradicate every single cancer cell in the body once spread has occurred. Unfortunately, by the time many people are aware of the fact that they have cancer the disease may be quite advanced because of this problem of spread. It is precisely for this reason that so much is written and said about early diagnosis. Women should learn how to examine their breasts properly and do so frequently, and everyone should have regular medical checkups, even if one is feeling in perfect health. And this is why it is so important to have persistent symptoms of any kind seen to by a doctor. In Question 8 we'll discuss cancer diagnosis and especially some of the ways of diagnosing some types of cancer very early.

Let's examine in greater detail this problem of cancer cells spreading to other parts of the body. Unfortunately, this can happen very soon after a cancer begins to grow. As I indicated a moment ago, no part of the body is protected from invasion by a growing cancer. Therefore, cancer cells are able to invade the tiny blood vessels that are present everywhere in the body. When this happens, some of the cancer cells are actually swept into the bloodstream and travel in the circulating blood. Since the blood circulates through the entire body, individual cancer cells can be deposited in many different organs. In these new locations the cancer cells begin to grow essentially as new cancers in exactly the same way they grew in the part of the body where they originated. Once again they increase in number and infiltrate into the surrounding tissues. This process is called *metastasis* and the growths are called *metastases* (from the Greek words *meta*, meaning "after" or "beyond," and *stasis*, meaning "stand"); literally then, a metastasis is a second stand or later appearance of cancer. There are no rules about the number of these secondary growths or where they grow. Metastases may be limited to a few selected places, or they may be rampant in many organs or tissues. The lungs, brain, liver, and bones are particularly frequent sites to which cancer cells spread.

To make things even more difficult, travel through the blood is not the only way in which cancer cells can spread. There is a second circulation in the body. Like the blood circulation, it consists of a vast network of tiny vessels, except that instead of transporting blood, this second circulation transports a liquid called *lymph* that constantly bathes the tissues of the body. So this circulatory system of vessels is called the *lymphatic system*. Located at various intervals along the lymphatic circulation, much like stations on a long railroad line, are little structures called *lymph nodes* (or *lymph glands*) where the lymph gets filtered and purified. In the same way that cancer cells can invade and puncture the walls of tiny blood vessels, they can also find their way into lymphatic vessels and be swept into the lymphatic circulation. In this case, instead of being transported to various organs in the body, they are transported to the nearest lymph node "stations" and begin to grow in them, causing them to become enlarged.

Metastasis to lymph nodes is a very frequent means of spread of cancer, so much so that it is not at all uncommon to discover a cancer because it has spread to the neighboring lymph nodes, causing

18

them to become enlarged, before the primary site of the cancer is discovered. Once again breast cancer provides an informative example. If cells from a very small cancer in the breast find their way into the lymphatic vessels the cells will often travel to lymph nodes in the armpit, one of the lymph node "stations" near the breast. When these lymph nodes become enlarged because of the growth of cancer cells they can actually be felt as discrete hard lumps in the armpit. Many cancers of the breast are discovered by first discovering enlarged lymph nodes in the armpit, either by the patient herself or by her doctor during a routine checkup. Similarly, a cancer growing in the throat, where it might be difficult to see and certainly very difficult to feel, can spread quite quickly to lymph nodes in the neck, and the enlarged nodes might be the problem that is discovered first.

The spread of cancer to the lymph nodes can increase the chances of the cancer spreading to other parts of the body. This can happen in two ways. First, the lymphatic circulation eventually empties into the blood circulation, much like one major river joining another. So cancer cells that spread through the lymphatic system will ultimately enter the bloodstream and spread around the body. Second, when cancer cells grow in a lymph gland they eventually break through the node and by the relentless process of invasion move into the surrounding tissues. There are thousands of tiny lymph nodes scattered all over the body, and as any of them become occupied by cancer cells each affected lymph node constitutes a possible new center of metastatic growth from which further spread of the disease can occur.

In summary, cancer cells in any organ or tissue of the body can metastasize to other organs and tissues through the blood circulation and through the lymphatic circulation. And because they can grow in different, sometimes numerous organs at the same time, it is easy to understand how eventually the functions of these organs can become adversely affected. And that is how cancer, the process of uncontrolled growth of cells, causes a progressive deterioration of health and, in many cases, death. This is the nature and dimension of the problem that must be dealt with in order to rid the body of cancer. As you will discover in Question 18, we are getting better and better every day in successfully attacking this problem.

What's the difference between a cancer and a tumor?

4

The two are the same,
but after they are produced,
they have different names.

—Lao-tzu

As I explained in Question 2, not every lump or bump that is unexpectedly discovered in the shower is necessarily cancer. As you have no doubt discovered through your own experience, lumps and bumps and swellings of all types are extremely common. We call them *tumors* (from the Latin for "swelling" or "distension"), and they can happen for all sorts of reasons that have nothing to do with the uncontrolled growth of cells. If you have ever been bitten by a spider you will certainly remember the rapid development of a hot, painful swelling where you were bitten. Or you may have experienced a relatively harmless large swollen bruise under the skin, called a *hematoma,* perhaps following a fall, or after having had blood drawn for a blood test or after donating blood at a transfusion center. No one calls insect bites or hematomas tumors, but by strict medical definition they are.

Unfortunately, some lumps and bumps are due to the uncontrolled growth of cells: cancer. But now that you are becoming more sophisticated in your understanding of cancer we should begin to use more accurate terms. The correct name for a swelling that is caused by the uncontrolled growth of cells is *neoplasm* (from the Greek words for "new" and "formation" or "growth"). Because most of us don't run off to see a doctor when we know full well that the swelling on Billy's leg is a spider bite or the place where he got kicked playing football, neoplasms are the most common and certainly the most serious swellings that doctors encounter. For this reason over the years doctors have come to use the terms *neoplasm* and *tumor* more or less interchangeably. So let's follow this popular convention. From now on "tumor" is what we'll call a collection of cells that develops as the result of the uncontrolled growth of cells somewhere in the body. (But if you want to be very smart, the next time your neighbor shows you a particularly nasty mosquito bite tell him it's really a non-neoplastic tumor!)

Let's clarify a few more important terms. Some tumors are of course made up of cancer cells. These are called *malignant* tumors (from the Latin for "malicious"—a very appropriate description of this destructive disease). Malignant tumors, and only these tumors, have the special ability that we discussed earlier of invading the surrounding tissues and spreading by metastasis to various parts of the body.

But many tumors do not invade or metastasize even though they are still neoplasms. In other words, like malignant tumors they develop because of the uncontrolled growth of cells, but they do not acquire the special properties that cause cells to spread and that have such devastating consequences for our health. We call these tumors *benign* (from the Latin for "well"). We will discuss some of the differences between benign and malignant tumors with some examples of common benign tumors, in Question 5.

Are you confused? Don't be. It's quite simple really. The terms *cancer, malignant neoplasm,* and *tumor* are used interchangeably. Just remember that "tumor" needs to be qualified. She has a tumor in her breast. Oh dear! Is it a benign tumor (not cancer) or is it a malignant tumor (cancer)? Soon you will learn that the word "cancer" itself is also considered to be colloquial, and I'll introduce a more accurate vocabulary for talking about and hence distinguishing between different types of cancer. It's important for you to know at least some of these names because doctors—especially those who specialize in the diagnosis and treatment of cancer (*oncologists*)—

tend to forget that most people don't speak the same language they do. One way of dealing with this problem is to forthrightly say "Wait a moment, doctor, I don't understand that word." But it certainly will help your discussions if you do understand some of these terms. (And don't forget the glossary at the end of the book in case you need to refer to the meaning of these words again.)

What's the difference between benign and malignant?

5

Like—but oh! how different.
              —Wordsworth

As I've already mentioned, the most important difference between benign and malignant tumors is that malignant tumors can spread to many different parts of the body, while benign tumors *never* do. That's why it is such a tremendous relief to know that a swelling or lump that one was worried about is benign. But benign tumors are genuine neoplasms—that is, they consist of cells in which growth is not properly regulated and they grow progressively. Most of them grow very slowly with a relative lack of seriousness in terms of one's health. For example, many women lead perfectly healthy lives with benign tumors of the womb (called *fibroids*), and thousands of perfectly healthy people have benign tumors of the fatty tissue under the skin (called *lipomas*), frequently on the back. Common warts and moles are also examples of benign tumors of the skin.

We do not understand why the cells of a benign tumor do not spread or invade, while the cells of a malignant tumor do. Despite the fact that benign tumors don't spread, they can cause serious disease and even death if they grow in a vital organ such as the brain or the heart. But because they never spread, most benign tumors are not harmful and their removal almost always results in a complete cure. In fact, it isn't always necessary to remove benign tumors at all unless they are growing in places where they might cause problems, or are cosmetically bothersome.

Can benign
tumors
become
malignant?

Q

6

Since 'tis Nature's law to change,
Constancy alone is strange.
                                    —*John Wilmot*

Some benign tumors can and quite frequently do undergo malignant change, but this is not the case with most of them. A notable example is a type of benign tumor of the large bowel called an *intestinal polyp*. Intestinal polyps can eventually become malignant, giving rise to cancer of the large bowel (cancer of the colon). You might remember that President Reagan had such polyps removed from his colon as a precautionary measure. Cancer of the colon is one of the most common forms of cancer in both men and women. Because of the fact that benign intestinal polyps can change to a malignant state, giving rise to cancer of the colon, it makes obvious sense to have periodic checkups with one's doctor to determine whether or not one has intestinal polyps. Nowadays this involves a relatively simple and relatively painless procedure during which the large intestine (colon) is carefully examined by passing a tube with special optics (called an *proctoscope*) into the colon through the rectum. If intestinal polyps are found, the same instrument allows for a small sample of the tumor to be removed for special examination. In fact, in some cases, the entire polyp can be removed at that time.

Some people are born with an increased risk of developing intestinal polyps; they can have thousands of them in their colon. This is an especially serious situation, since any one of these polyps can become cancerous. We'll discuss the importance of inherited predisposition to cancer in more detail in Question 16 when we talk about hereditary risks of cancer.

On occasion other types of benign tumors can become malignant. A type you should be particularly aware of are the pigmented moles that many of us have on our skin. We all have a variety of pigmented spots. The great majority are simple freckles, which are collections of cells deep in the skin that contain a brown pigment called *melanin.* This pigment is present in cells all over the skin, and it is very important in protecting our skin from the harmful effects of sunlight.

But in addition to freckles we can have other small brown or black spots that most of us simply call moles. Sometimes these form a discrete little swelling or tumor in the skin. There are actually several different kinds of moles, and most of them are perfectly harmless and benign. But very occasionally some of them can become cancerous, giving rise to a very serious type of malignant tumor called a *melanoma,* which can spread to other parts of the body extremely rapidly, even though it remains quite tiny in the skin. As I mentioned in Question 3, the things to watch for are any change in the behavior of a mole that you have had for a long time. If it changes its color, or bleeds often, or begins to get bigger, or itches frequently, you should certainly consult your doctor. You should also take special notice of any moles or pigmented spots on the palms of the hands, the soles of the feet, or the skin of the scrotum. For reasons that we don't understand, moles in these places have a tendency to become malignant more often.

But for the purposes of this discussion it is surely a relief to know that the majority of benign tumors *remain* benign. In other words, they never invade or spread. The majority of cancers (malignant tumors) do not first go through an extended benign stage. They are malignant from the beginning.

What's the difference between carcinoma, sarcoma, leukemia, and lymphoma?

7

Differing but in degree, of kind the same.
                                        —*John Milton*

We all recognize that appendicitis and pneumonia and meningitis are different diseases. But in fact they are all diseases caused by infections of one sort or another, and in this sense they can be thought of as different forms of a single disease entity, infection. The same is true of cancer. Cancer is not a single disease but rather a single disease *entity* comprising many different individual diseases or cancers. Virtually every cell type in the body can become cancerous. Depending on which particular cell does so, we give that type of cancer a different name. Why make it all so complicated? Well, one of the many reasons that it's worth giving an infection of the appendix (appendicitis) a different name from an infection of the lung (pneumonia) is that we treat them differently. We remove an infected appendix by a surgical operation. We treat an infected lung with antibiotics. In the same way that we consider appendicitis to be a different disease from pneumonia, especially from the point of view of its treatment, so one type of cancer can be very different from another.

There are many different types of cells in the body. Not surprisingly, therefore, there are many different types of cancer. In fact, in some organs one particular type of cell can give rise to more than one type of cancer. Since every cancer known has a different name, doctors have a rather extensive vocabulary when they discuss cancer. There is no need here to bother you with all these names. However, some of them are so common that it is virtually impossible to talk to any health professional or to read any literature about cancer without encountering them. So let me tell you something about the basic terminology for the naming of cancers.

The cells that line all the surfaces of the body are called *epithelial cells.* Of course the entire skin is a surface and is covered by a sheet of epithelial cells called the *epithelium.* But there are lots of other surfaces in the body that are perhaps less obvious to you. For example, epithelial cells line the inside of the mouth and nose, the stomach and intestines, and the miles of passages through which air passes into the lungs, to name just a few. The female breast is composed of a network of tiny little tubes through which milk is carried to the nipple during breast feeding. These tubes, which increase in size and in number during and immediately after pregnancy, are also lined with epithelial cells. And finally, we call the cells in many of the organs of the body epithelial cells. For example, the liver and kidneys consist mainly of these cells. So there are many different epithelial cells in the body.

When epithelial cells anywhere in the body become cancerous we call such cancers *carcinomas* (from the Greek *karkinos,* which like the Latin *cancer,* means "crab" and *oma,* a suffix meaning "tumor"). So, when we talk of *carcinoma of the lung* we mean a malignant tumor that develops because of cancerous changes in cells lining the air passages. Similarly, when we talk of *carcinoma of the colon,* we mean a malignant tumor of cells lining the inside of the large intestine. Since we have a special name for malignant tumors of epithelial cells you might imagine that we also have a special name for benign tumors of these cells. Indeed we do. We call such tumors *adenomas.* So, other names for the benign polyps of the intestine that we discussed earlier are adenomas of the colon or adenomatous polyps of the colon.

Carcinomas are the most common forms of cancer. Another common type of cancer is called *leukemia,* a term that I'm sure you are familiar with. As I have already mentioned, blood circulates to every part of the body through an elaborate system of blood vessels. It contains two major types of cells: *red blood cells* and *white blood cells*. These cells are fed into the blood from special parent cells in the bone marrow that constantly divide and give rise to the red and white blood cells.

When white blood cells become cancerous they give rise to leukemia (from the Greek *leukos,* meaning "white" and *haima,* meaning "blood"). There are several different types of white blood cells and so there are several different types of leukemia. The soft center part of our bones is called the marrow. *Bone marrow* is soft and pulpy because it contains large numbers of cells that are in various stages of maturation to fully formed red and white blood cells, which are then released into the bloodstream. Leukemias actually develop from the cells in the bone marrow that give rise to white blood cells, rather than from the mature white blood cells themselves. So, in effect, leukemias are actually cancers of the bone marrow. But leukemia is different from true bone cancer, which develops from cells (not marrow cells) that make up the bone itself. As you will see in a moment, bone cancer has a name of its own.

A particular type of white blood cell is also present in the lymphatic system which we talked about in Question 3. These white blood cells are called *lymphocytes* and the lymph nodes (those little stations along the track of lymphatic vessels) contain many of them. When these cells become cancerous we call the cancer *lymphoma.* There are several different types of lymphomas too, depending on which particular type of lymphocyte becomes cancerous.

Having dealt with carcinomas, leukemias, and lymphomas we have in fact dealt with the great majority of cancers. So what cells in the body are left? Outside of the organs and the blood cells we can consider most of the rest of the body to be composed of a scaffold or general support structure consisting of the bones (the true scaffold or skeleton), the muscles, fat, blood vessels, nerves, and a special type of tissue that we call *connective tissue.* Most of the connective tissue in the body consists of a delicate sheet of white tissue with a fibrous consistency which is present immediately underneath the epithelial linings of the body, and connects the epithelium to deeper tissues, such as muscles for example. The next time you are eating a chicken leg you might want to examine the tissue immediately under the skin which connects the skin to the actual meat. That's a very good example of connective tissue.

Ligaments and tendons are an example of a special type of connective tissue. They connect the muscles to the bones and are the white fibrous stuff that is always difficult to chew and swallow in an otherwise tender steak. As I have already indicated, connective tissue is quite fibrous in its consistency; for this reason cells that are present in connective tissue are called *fibroblasts.*

Cancers that arise from cells in this general body scaffold are called *sarcomas,* (from the Greek *sarkos,* meaning "flesh"). Because the body scaffold consists of the many different types of tissues described above, we give sarcomas from each of these tissues specific names. For example, we call a cancer from bone cells an *osteosarcoma* (from the Greek *osteon,* meaning "bone"), and we call a cancer from muscle cells the awful tongue twister, *rhabdomyosarcoma* (pronounced with a silent *h*), derived from the Greek *rhabdos* meaning "rod," and *myo,* meaning "muscle." Muscle cells do indeed have a long rodlike shape when looked at under a microscope. (This is the type of cancer that Dave Dravecky, the pitcher with the San Francisco Giants, had).

The following table lists the names of the most common sarcomas and the cells from which they are derived. You may want to come back to this list at some point to see how most of the common sarcomas are named. The table also shows the names of benign tumors of these tissues.

The types of cancer we've discussed—carcinomas, leukemias, lymphomas and the various sarcomas—account for more than 95

Sarcomas Are Tumors of Supporting Tissues

Malignant Tumor	Benign Tumor	Cell Of Origin
Osteosarcoma	Osteoma	Bone cells
Rhabdomyosarcoma	Rhabdomyoma	Muscle cells
Fibrosarcoma	Fibroma	Fibroblasts
Liposarcoma	Lipoma	Fat cells
Chondrosarcoma	Chondroma	Cartilage cells
Angiosarcoma	Angioma	Blood vessel cells

percent of all human cancers. But an important point to remember is that because every organ consists of different cell types, that organ can be the seat of several different types of cancers. In order to be sure that we communicate properly when we talk about all these different cancers it's often important to use their correct names. If one simply talks about "cancer of the colon," one could be talking about a cancer of the epithelial cells of the colon (*carcinoma of the colon*), or of connective tissue cells of the colon (*fibrosarcoma of the colon*), or even of muscle cells in the colon (*leiomyosarcoma of the colon*). In fact, most cancers of the colon happen to be carcinomas.

How is cancer
diagnosed?

8

Certain signs predict certain events.

—*Cicero*

The earlier any cancer is diagnosed the sooner treatment can begin and the better the outlook for the patient. So a lot of attention is justifiably given to early diagnosis by various cancer agencies. Unfortunately, it is not yet possible to diagnose every type of cancer at a stage before it has spread to other parts of the body. But increasingly, more and better ways of diagnosing at least some forms of cancer are being discovered. Let's talk a little about some of these.

You are probably familiar with the conventional X-ray examination whereby organs, and especially bones, can be examined in considerable detail. Cancers in many parts of the body that cannot be easily felt can be seen on an X-ray film. But in recent years spectacular advances have been made in other types of imaging techniques that allow the detection of cancers which cannot even be seen with conventional X-rays. These diagnostic procedures have a variety of names depending on what technique is actually being used, including *CAT* (*c*omputerized *a*xial *t*omography) *scanning,* a very sophisticated computerized imaging technique; *MRI* (*m*agnetic *r*esonance *i*maging), a technique that uses a strong magnetic field; and *ultrasound,* a technique that uses sound waves instead of X-rays to make an image of organs and tissues. In fact ultrasound is so safe and so accurate it is now routinely used for examining babies in the womb, so that abnormalities that might develop during pregnancy can be seen.

A very special type of X-ray examination of the breast called a *mammogram*, has been extremely helpful in diagnosing many cases of early breast cancer. It is recommended that every woman have their first mammogram no later than age 35 to 39. This is called a base-line mammogram against which all subsequent ones can be compared to see if any changes have occurred. After the age of 40 women should have routine mammograms every other year, and after the age of 50 every year. Nancy Brinker of the Susan G. Komen Breast Cancer Foundation has recently written an extremely informative and readable book on all aspects of breast cancer, including its early diagnosis. For details, see the section on recommended further reading.

Some cancer cells produce substances that normal cells don't make, or the cancer cells produce substances in higher amounts than normal. Almost all substances that cells make eventually find their way into the blood. So drawing a small amount of blood and carrying out special chemical tests on it sometimes allows certain types of cancer to be diagnosed, or at least suspected. For example, the *prostate gland* is a small organ located near the base of the bladder in men. It produces a substance that is necessary for sperm to function normally, so it is required for fertility. Unfortunately, when many men are long past the age when fertility has much relevance, this little gland is a rather frequent place for cancer to develop. A particular substance made by cells in the prostate gland, called *prostate specific antigen* (*PSA*) can be a very useful blood test for the early diagnosis of cancer of the prostate. We'll talk more about cancer of the prostate in Question 13.

The definitive determination that cancer is present in any part of the body and the diagnosis of the particular type of cancer are usually made by removing a small amount of the tumor and examining it under a microscope. This process is called *biopsy* (from the Greek *bio*, meaning "life" and *opsis*, meaning "vision")—in other words the examination of living tissues. Biopsies are usually carried out even if the physician is fairly certain that a cancer is present, because as I mentioned before different tumors are treated differently, and it is extremely important to know exactly what type of tumor is present in order to plan effective treatment. We will talk more about the different treatments of cancer later in the book.

If a tumor is easily accessible, for example in the breast, or somewhere in or just under the skin, biopsy is a minor surgical procedure that typically requires nothing more than a local anesthetic. Modern medicine has made many other parts of the body quite accessible for biopsy purposes. Thanks to sophisticated instrumentation and optics, the throat, the gullet, the stomach, the bladder, the womb, parts of the intestines, and even the larger air passages in the lungs can all be safely explored for biopsy purposes without having to perform major surgery. In some cases it is possible to biopsy a tumor by simply sticking a very fine needle into the tissue and sucking out a tiny piece, a procedure called *fine needle aspiration* (*FNA*). If the tumor is located in the brain or in some other part of the body that's a little more difficult to reach, it is of course necessary to perform the biopsy in a formal operation under a general anesthetic.

Once a small piece of a tumor is removed it is carefully examined by a *pathologist,* a physician who is specially trained to recognize the "look" of cancer cells under a microscope, and who can also tell what particular type of cells the cancer came from and therefore give it the appropriate designation of carcinoma, sarcoma, and so on. As a pathologist myself I was rather dismayed to recently discover that a young relative of mine (a college student, no less), thought that pathologists were people who spent all their time cutting up dead bodies!

Sometimes the biopsy and hence formal diagnosis of cancer and its treatment by surgical removal are carried out at the same time. The patient is given a general anesthetic in the operating room and an operation is carried out to biopsy the tumor. The biopsy is immediately handed to a pathologist at a work station just outside the operating theater. In this type of situation the pathologist uses a process specially designed to provide a diagnosis within a matter of minutes. The process employs the rapid freezing of the tissue so that it can be cut into very thin slices (or sections) for examination under the microscope. So this procedure is called a *frozen section*. If cancer is identified by frozen section the surgeon will frequently go ahead and remove it there and then, provided that it is operable. Let's defer discussing the difference between operable and inoperable cancer until Question 18 when we talk about cancer treatment in greater detail.

For certain types of cancer a definitive diagnosis sometimes includes an evaluation of the extent of the tumor. A good example is lymphoma, which as I mentioned earlier, is a tumor derived from cells called lymphocytes, which are present in the lymph nodes. Since we all have thousands of lymph nodes distributed all over the body, lymphoma can strike multiple sites simultaneously. In order to plan treatment effectively it is important to establish precisely how many places in the body are affected by the disease. The best way of doing this is to operate on the patient in order to directly examine different lymph nodes in the belly. This procedure of surgically evaluating the extent of lymphoma is called *staging*. A stage 1 lymphoma (meaning that the lymphoma is localized to a particular part of the body) may require one type of treatment, but a stage 4 lymphoma (meaning that the cancer is present in more than one part of the body) may require a different type of treatment. Staging is sometimes applied to the diagnosis of other types of cancer (see Question 13).

What are my chances of developing cancer and dying from it?

9

*The laws of probability, so true in general,
so fallacious in particular.*

—*Edward Gibbon*

The disheartening but honest answer to this question is that one's chance of developing cancer and dying from it sometime in one's life are rather high. Any child born in the United States in 1985 has a more than one in three chance of eventually developing some form of invasive cancer and about 1 in 5 deaths in the United States are the result of this disease entity.

Quite understandably, people tend to misinterpret statistics because statistics can be quite confusing, sometimes even to experts. So I want to be sure that you understand exactly what we mean when we talk about a particular risk of getting cancer or of dying of cancer. Let's consider, for example, the statistical fact that in most Western countries 1 out of every 9 women develop breast cancer. This figure is alarming to many women because it suggests to them that among a group of themselves plus another eight relatives or friends, one of them is definitely going to get breast cancer. And when people are alarmed about getting cancer they don't think about the disease in terms of the next ten years or twenty years. They tend to think of getting it next month or next year. But this figure of 1 in 9 does not apply to next month or next year. It is really the *cumulative* risk of getting breast cancer over one's entire life. More accurately, it is the risk of getting breast cancer sometime between the time of birth and the age of 110. If you are under the age of 50, the risk of getting breast cancer *next year* is realistically closer to 1 in

1000, and your risk of actually *dying* from breast cancer is still lower. This is still a considerable risk. And of course the risk of 1 in 5 of dying from one of the many different types of cancers sometime in one's life indicates that cancer is indeed a common and dangerous disease. But remember to get more detailed information about the cancer statistics that you read and hear about, and keep them in correct perspective with respect to other risks in life. For example, it has been estimated that if you are about 40 years old, your risk of dying of breast cancer *next year* is about 1 in 1000. (But it is also true that your risk of dying in a car accident next year is about 1 in 5000.)

Let's consider some other well-documented and rather sobering cancer statistics. During the year 1987 (the year for which the most recent statistics are available), there were more than two million registered deaths in the United States. Cancer was the second leading cause of death after heart diseases and accounted for over 476,000 deaths, or more than 22 percent of the fatalities from all causes.

In the year 1987 more than 16,000 deaths from all causes in the United States involved children between the ages of 1 and 14. Almost half of these were the result of accidents of one sort or another. Children are not at risk for diseases such as heart attacks, that kill older people. After accidents, the leading cause of death in children is cancer, which accounted for nearly 1,700 deaths of children in 1987. Cancer is the second leading cause of death both in adults and in children.

These facts and figures are typical for many parts of the world. In order to make direct comparisons between one country and another it is more meaningful to compare cancer deaths that occur in the same number of people in the population. That way we don't have to worry about the different population sizes in different countries. During the period between 1984 and 1986 cancer accounted for approximately 357 deaths per 100,000 people in the United States. Very comparable numbers for the same three-year period come from cancer registries in many other countries in the

Estimated Cancer Percentages in the United States in 1991

Men		Women	
Type		*Type*	
Prostate	22	Breast	32
Lung	19	Colon and rectum	14
Colon and rectum	14	Lung	11
Bladder	10	Uterus	8
Leukemia and lymphoma	7	Leukemia and lymphoma	6
Mouth	4	Bladder	4
Stomach	3	Ovary	4
Pancreas	3	Pancreas	3
Melanoma of the skin	3	Melanoma of the skin	3
All other	15	Mouth	2
		All other	13
	100		100

world, including the United Kingdom, France, Germany, Scandinavia, and countries in South America.

Based on an analysis of a large number of cancer cases documented over many years, the National Cancer Institute, a federal agency specifically dedicated to the study of cancer and located at the National Institutes of Health in Bethesda, Maryland, estimated that there would be over a million *new* cases of cancer diagnosed in the United States in 1991. The table above shows the percentages of the most frequent cancers in men and women.

Notice that cancer of the lungs, colo-rectal cancer, and cancer of the prostate were expected to account for more than 50 percent of *all* cancers in men, and that cancer of the lung, colo-rectal cancer, and cancer of the breast were expected to account for more than 50 percent of *all* cancers in women. This estimate did not include the most common of all cancers, carcinoma of the skin, because in most cases this type of skin cancer can be completely cured if properly treated, and so for all practical purposes we can ignore it. It also excluded an extremely common early form of cancer of the cervix and very early breast cancer in women. These were left out of the prediction because when treated they also usually result in a complete cure. These particular forms of cancer comprise about another 700,000 new cases every year. But if we add them to the million other cases predicted by the National Cancer Institute, the total comes to 1,700,000. This works out to be one *new* case of cancer for about every 150 people in the United States *each year.*

Another way of looking at the frequency of different cancers is to ask which *particular* cancers kill people most commonly, among the *total* deaths from cancer. Of course, when we ask how many people actually die from different cancers the numbers not only tell us how common these cancers are, but also how effectively they are being treated. Let's examine these figures from several different countries, as shown in the following table.

We see that cancer of the lung, colon and rectum, breast, and prostate not only account for more than half of the total cancers, but they also account for over half of the deaths from cancer.

By comparing the death rates for different types of cancer in different parts of the world we find that in some countries particular cancers are more of a problem than in others. For example, in the United States about 42 people per 100,000 died of cancer of the colon and rectum during the period 1984 to 1986. But in New Zealand about 62 people per 100,000 died of this type of cancer, and in Ecuador only 9 per 100,000 did. Similarly, in England and Wales

Death Rates from Selected Cancers
During the Period 1984-1986

*Death Rate as a Percentage of Total Cancer Deaths
in Selected Countries*

Type of Cancer	United States	England/Wales	Netherlands	Canada
Lung	27.9	27.7	27.6	25.8
Colon and rectum	11.6	12.0	10.8	11.7
Breast	7.7	8.9	7.8	8.0
Prostate	6.5	5.5	6.3	6.5
Leukemia	3.8	2.8	2.9	3.6

36 women per 100,000 died of breast cancer, but in Ecuador only about 6 per 100,000 did. Assuming that there are no major differences in the diagnosis or treatment of cancer in these different countries, these very different death rates suggest that in different parts of the world there are different causative factors at work and also that differences in our genetic makeup may make us more or less susceptible to different cancers. We'll discuss this topic in more detail in Question 16. But now let's consider some of the factors in the environment that contribute to the development of cancer.

Why is cancer
so common?

10

Alas, our frailty is the cause, not we!
For such as we be made of, such we be.
—*William Shakespeare*

Before we attempt to examine this complicated question let's clarify some common conceptions and misconceptions. First, cancer is primarily (but not exclusively) a disease that results in disability and death in older people. The average age at which all cancers are diagnosed in most Westernized countries is between 60 and 65. Of the more than 469,000 documented cases of deaths due to cancer in 1986 in the United States, the great majority (close to 90 percent) involved persons older than 55. As life expectancy has progressively improved in the Western world because of improved nutrition and health care, and particularly because of the eradication of infectious diseases such as smallpox, more people are surviving to an age at which they are at risk for death from other diseases, particularly heart disease and cancer. The longer one lives the greater is the chance that one will eventually develop some form of cancer. Thousands of years ago our ancestors probably never got cancer because they were extremely fortunate if they survived to an age at which cancer was even a remote possibility. They had to worry about saber-toothed tigers and snakes and poisonous plants and infections. The price that you and I must pay for our much safer modern society is that we stand a very good chance of living to a ripe old age and therefore of getting cancer.

Why is it that as we get older we are at increasing risk for cancer? At one time physicians used to think that something about the process of aging might predispose us to cancer. It was suggested that older cells were more likely to undergo cancerous change than young cells just because they were older. More likely the significance of aging is the fact that during the many years of life certain critical events accumulate in some of our cells which can eventually lead to cancerous change. Let's explore some of the factors that might contribute to the frequency of these events, and hence increase the likelihood that some of our cells will become cancerous.

In recent years the popular press and the media in general have drawn a lot of attention to the role of the environment in the causation of cancer. Justifiably so. The world that we live in does contain harmful chemicals and other agents (such as radiation) that we know can cause cancer. But it is important to keep the role of the environment in cancer causation in a balanced perspective. There is little question that if you are exposed to high doses of cancer-causing agents (called *carcinogens*), your risk of getting cancer is increased. We don't need to rely on sophisticated laboratory tests in order to be convinced of this. There are numerous unfortunate examples in humans. One of the most dramatic recent examples was the discovery of a profound increase in the incidence of various types of cancer in people who were exposed to radiation from the atomic bomb explosions in Japan in World War II.

Another dramatic example of the relationship between environmental carcinogens and cancer comes from detailed studies on cigarette smokers. Regardless of what advocates of the tobacco industry and others with vested interests might tell you, if you smoke cigarettes your risk of getting lung cancer is definitely increased. The extent of the risk obviously depends on just how much you smoke, and on a variety of other factors. But in general the risk is anywhere from ten to fifty times higher than that of a nonsmoker. Consider that in the year 1990, more than 30 percent of the cancer-related deaths in men, and more than 20 percent of the cancer-related deaths in women in the United States were from lung cancer. In Scotland during the period 1984 to 1986 more than 39 percent of the total cancer-related deaths in men were from lung cancer. There is now increasing evidence that passive smoking—the inhalation of cigarette smoke generated by a smoker in the same room—also increases one's risk of lung cancer. This is the cost of cigarette smoking.

There are many other well-studied and unambiguous examples of environmentally related cancers. In fact, historically the observation that exposure to certain kinds of environmental agents increases the risk of cancer provided the first clues about some of the types of chemicals that can cause cancer. A little over two hundred years ago a British surgeon by the name of Percival Pott made the observation that many men with cancer of the skin or of the scrotum were chimney sweeps when they were young boys. In England during the late eighteenth century an effective (and certainly a cheap) way of cleaning chimneys was to lower a child armed with a long brush down a chimney. When he emerged at the other end, so did a lot of the soot that was clogging the chimney. Aside from the fact that they were not protected by labor laws in those days, the chief reason for using children for this purpose was that they could easily fit down most chimneys!

The soot that accumulates in chimneys and in other places where coal is burnt contains very potent carcinogens. In fact, we now know that some of these very same carcinogens are produced when tobacco is burnt, and are therefore inhaled during cigarette smoking. They are also released in automobile exhaust emissions. So, constant contamination with soot, together with the fact that children (and in those days most adults) took baths rather infrequently, and probably washed their genitals less frequently than their hands and face, presumably led to an accumulation of soot around the scrotum, and, eventually, to cancer in some men.

This was a rather remarkable observation by Dr. Pott, because two hundred years ago very little indeed was known about the causation of cancer. There were no cancer statistics of the type that I have just quoted to you, so there really was no particular reason to suspect that cancer had anything at all to do with chemicals, or the environment. For all that was known about human disease in 1775, cancer could have been caused by evil spirits! Shortly after Dr. Pott described his findings to a scientific organization in England the Danish chimney sweepers' guild heard about his study and urged its members to take frequent baths. Not too surprising to us now, but certainly surprising for that time in history, within about twenty years a large drop in the incidence of scrotal cancer was noted in chimney sweeps in northern Europe compared to the incidence in England where they continued to bathe infrequently. This probably represents the first effective public health measure in the prevention of human cancer.

The documented association of certain cancers with particular environmental situations is now a formal discipline in the study of cancer and is called *cancer epidemiology*. It is an extremely important way of tracking down and identifying particular carcinogens in the general environment and the workplace and has played a very big role in associating cancer of the lung with exposure to asbestos in people who handle asbestos occupationally, and numerous other examples of what we call occupational cancer—cancer for which there is a high risk due to particular kinds of exposure during work.

Just how dangerous is the environment? There is little doubt that if you were a survivor of the Chernobyl nuclear accident in Russia you should be justifiably worried about getting some type of cancer. As I have just indicated, you should also be justifiably worried about developing lung cancer if you work in an asbestos processing plant without adequate protection, or if you smoke heavily. But what about your risk of cancer if you have a dental X-ray once a year and you eat and drink a reasonably well-balanced diet (but including the occasional charbroiled hamburger and maraschino cherry), and live in an industrial city and must endure exhaust pollution from cars and buses?

The best estimates based on the study of thousands of people who have been exposed to all kinds of environmental agents (such as routine X-rays) is that low-level exposure to environmental agents in the course of normal lifestyles does not make a *major* contribution to the incidence of cancer. The best evidence for this comes from studies that have followed the incidence of cancer and the frequency of deaths due to cancer over many years. Let's briefly consider the death rate in the United States over the past sixty years from several common cancers. Statistics for many thousands of cases show that since 1930 lung cancer is the only common cancer for which the death rate has increased progressively, almost certainly because of cigarette smoking. However, in both men and women the death rate from leukemia and from cancer of the colon, bladder, liver, and ovary has remained essentially unchanged for the past fifty years. Indeed, deaths due to cancer of the stomach have actually declined rather dramatically and in women deaths from cancer of the uterus and cervix have also decreased.

Let's ignore for the moment the intriguing question as to why these cancers have actually decreased as causes of death. The point I want to make here is that they certainly have not *increased* over the past fifty years. In other words, there is no good evidence that we live in a world that is flooded with dangerous levels of cancer-causing agents, as some people believe. Nor is there reliable evidence that modern industry is increasingly and uncaringly promoting a serious general risk to our health as far as cancer is concerned. The sober reality is that even though there are lots of very good reasons for keeping our environment well controlled, some which are certainly related to human health and well-being in general, preventing cancer is not one of the most critical.

This is most certainly not to say that the general environment poses no risk at all for cancer. Nor is it to say that in some parts of the world environmental exposure due to industrial pollution does not create significant risks for populations exposed to high levels of particular carcinogens. But some sort of perspective must be maintained. While it is undeniably true that burnt charcoal contains carcinogens, it is a fallacy to believe that you will not get cancer of the stomach if you decide to never again eat anything that was cooked over a charcoal fire. In the final analysis you must understand that when we talk about factors which can cause cancer we are really talking about *risks* of cancer. Smoking increases the risk of getting lung cancer and it is most certainly wise not to smoke. But not all cigarette smokers get lung cancer. In fact nine out of ten don't. And many people who get lung cancer never smoked a cigarette in their life. So clearly the causation of cancer is a complicated business that involves the interplay of multiple factors. Later in the book we'll discuss some of these other factors.

Well, if the environments that are products of modern industrialized societies are not major contributors to cancer incidence, why is cancer so common? In this regard there are two important considerations that you should keep in mind. First, let's dwell further on the topic of cancer-causing chemicals in the environment. We have a tendency to think that carcinogens are exclusively the products of industry, but this is not true. The great majority of chemicals in the world (including those that cause cancer) do not come from factories, they exist naturally. They exist as a part of the world of fruits and vegetables that so many of us have been eating for years, often in the very hope of protecting our bodies against the ravages of cancer. Many of these chemicals evolved in plants precisely because they are poisonous to normal cellular processes. That's how a potato plant (among many other plants and vegetables) protects itself from being eaten by insect predators.

We worry a lot about the use of artificial pesticides, but in fact some of the natural pesticides present in vegetables are not only powerful carcinogens, but are present in far higher amounts than could possibly be achieved by the spraying of crops. You might be amazed to know that if you are consuming a typical diet, 99.9 percent of the pesticides in your diet are natural and come from the fruit and vegetables that you eat. In other words we consume about ten thousand times more natural pesticides than manmade pesticides. Not too long ago a species of potato was developed that required no pesticides of any sort to protect it from insects. How wonderful, you might think, the perfect organic potato. Surely nothing could be more appropriate to grace the dinner table? Not so. This potato was so loaded with poisons it could have killed a full-grown adult if eaten in normal quantities; hence, it was withdrawn from the market. In a similar vein a strain of celery was produced that was highly insect resistant. This celery contained more than ten times the level of a well-known carcinogen present in "normal" strains. Fortunately, attention was drawn to this problem because this particular carcinogenic chemical is quite irritating to the skin and many people who handled the celery developed skin rashes. So one reason that the synthetic world may not significantly affect the incidence of human cancer is that the natural world may already be quite full of carcinogens.

Of course, I am not in the least suggesting that eating fruits and vegetables is bad for you. On the contrary, fruits and vegetables are loaded with vitamins and other goodies that our bodies absolutely require for all sorts of normal functions. As we will see in Question 15, fruits and vegetables also contain chemicals that we think might protect us against cancer. My point is simply that because something is natural it does not necessarily follow that it is free of dangerous chemicals. The dangerous chemicals in fruits and vegetables have evolved to do particular jobs that are useful to the plant. The fact that they can also cause cancer in people is unfortunate.

Believe it or not, another important source of natural carcinogens are our very own cells. Like other living things we also make chemicals in our body. But unlike plants, the chemicals we manufacture that can cause cancer are not intended for some other important function. They are actually the waste products of many of the chemical reactions that go on in our cells all the time. As life-forms that depend on oxygen we have evolved a particular type of metabolism that produces waste products which are capable of causing cancer. In Question 12 we will see exactly how these metabolic waste products work to cause cancer.

The second important consideration about cancer is that in many instances—perhaps in most instances—there is no identifiable cause of the disease. Cancer is extremely common. Assuming for the sake of argument that more than half of all human cancer could be prevented by banning the sale of cigarettes and eating a diet that was guaranteed to be carcinogen-free, instead of one in three people getting cancer maybe one in ten people or maybe only one in twenty would get the disease. But a disease that affects one in twenty people is still a very common disease and it would likely continue to rank as the second largest cause of death in the United States.

What accounts for the cancer cases that could probably not be prevented by any kind of environmental regulation? Fundamentally, cancer results from a breakdown of normal control mechanisms, the programs that control the orderly growth of cells. The fact that cancer is so common creates the impression that these controls don't work very well. But think for a moment about the incidence of cancer at the level of individual *cells* rather than individual *people*. As I indicated earlier, an incidence of 1.7 million cases of cancer a year means that each year roughly one in every one hundred and fifty people develops a cancer somewhere in their body. But remember that each person consists of about three trillion cells. Since every case of cancer starts in a single cell, the chance that any one cell will become cancerous in the total population of the United States in any one year is much, much, much smaller than one in one hundred and fifty; it is about one in a quadrillion. A quadrillion is a thousand trillion—in miles this is a distance farther than the most remote star to be seen from our solar system.

So quite clearly, most of the time the exquisitely complicated controls for normal cell growth work extremely well. But nature is not absolutely perfect, and every once in a while something goes wrong quite spontaneously and cells become cancerous. This is the price we have to pay for the fact that over millions of years we have evolved to be large life-forms consisting of many, many millions of cells and that we live for a rather long time; more than 70 years on the average.

The process of biological evolution is supposed to provide a continual selection in favor of situations that are advantageous to the survival of a species. So why, you might reasonably ask, during the millions of years of evolution did our cells not evolve ways of avoiding the problems that we have just discussed which make us vulnerable to cancer? Why didn't we develop a perfect resistance to natural carcinogens? Why didn't our cells learn to make waste products that don't cause cancer or learn to get rid of these waste products before they cause problems? And even though the way in which normal cell growth is regulated is satisfactory, why did it not become even better, so that it *never* breaks down to result in uncontrolled growth? The answer to these questions is that natural selection during evolution operates only if there is an advantage that can be enjoyed by an entire species of life-forms. If cancer mainly killed people when they were young the very existence of humans on the planet would be threatened because many people would not live long enough to have offspring. In that case the evolution of mechanisms for preventing cancer would have a strong selective advantage for the entire species of human beings. But since most people who die of cancer are too old to have any more offspring, it really doesn't make any difference to the survival of the species. So in effect there is no selection operating.

What causes
cells to become
cancerous?

11

*If you can look into the seeds of time and say
which will grow, and which will not,
speak then to me.*

—*William Shakespeare*

We have talked about the fact that certain agents we call *carcinogens* can increase the risk of cancer: artificial (synthetic) chemicals present in the environment, natural chemicals, even the products of the chemistry of our own cells. How do they do this? We don't know exactly what happens to normal cells to make them cancerous. This is a most intensive area of cancer research nowadays and great strides have been made with this problem, especially in the past ten years or so. This book is not intended to be a course in biology. But in order to understand something about the way cells become cancerous you need to understand some aspects of the basic biology of cells. Even though you are not a biologist, you might find it useful to know something about where we stand in the crusade against cancer. And wouldn't you like to know how much progress has been achieved in cancer research, and how your tax dollars that support such research are being spent? So stay with me—it's fascinating stuff and I promise you that I'll keep it simple and brief so that we can get back to answering more questions about the primary topic of this book.

Think about every cell in the body as a compartmentalized little factory in which hundreds of different activities are carried out by hundreds of machines. These machines do all sorts of things. They manufacture the bricks and mortar to make new cells. They control the normal growth of cells. They manufacture chemicals that are used to make energy so that we have the fuel to walk and run and think and breathe and do all the other things that we take for granted as living organisms. Many of these machines are the same in all cells in the body. They are used for the many routine things that all cells have to do, such as making energy. Some of the machines are different in different cells. For example, a liver cell makes some machines that are required only in liver cells, and muscle cells make certain machines that are used only in muscle cells. That's why liver cells and muscle cells do different things and look different under the microscope.

The machines are made up of a substance called *protein*. All cells have some protein machines in common, but in addition different types of cells manufacture different proteins, so that some of the proteins a liver cell makes are different from those that a muscle cell or a bone cell makes. Cells can also manufacture different protein machines at different times in order to do certain jobs that are only needed at a particular time. So the cellular factories manufacture protein machines that do all the general and specialized work that goes on in the body. These machines are therefore critical instruments for normal cellular function. Understandably, if one of these proteins is defective, that machine may become faulty or completely nonfunctional. When this happens to certain types of protein machines cells can become cancerous.

Now it would seem to follow that liver cells know how to make liver cell proteins but they don't know how to make muscle cell or bone cell proteins. Not true. It turns out that every cell in the body has the ability to make every type of protein. Liver cells do know how to make muscle cell proteins and bone cell proteins, but they normally don't. In other words, different cells are selective about which protein machines they normally make. So how do they achieve this extraordinary selectivity in different cells, and how is it that a particular type of cell can make different protein machines at different times?

Cells follow strict instructions that specify the manufacture of individual proteins. These instructions are stored in a very important substance called *DNA*, a material that I'm sure you've heard of or read about. The DNA of every cell contains about fifty thousand instructional units called *genes*. Each gene provides the instructions required to manufacture one protein in the cell. Every cell in the body has exactly the same amount of DNA and the same fifty thousand genes. That's the reason that every cell possesses the basic instructions for making every one of the thousands of different proteins in the entire body. Since the protein machines are responsible for all the activities that cells are engaged in, and since the specific instructions for making each protein come from the genes of DNA, you can appreciate why it is that DNA is sometimes called the master molecule, or the blueprint of life.

Different types of cells selectively use only the instructions in the particular set of genes for the particular set of proteins that they need. Imagine that every one of the fifty thousand genes in the DNA of each cell has a switch. Each cell knows how to turn certain switches to the ON position in order to read the instructions for making certain proteins, and how to switch other genes to the OFF position so that their instructions are not read. All cells switch on the genes that provide instructions for the routine general functions that we spoke about earlier, the functions that allow them to make energy, for example. But a liver cell additionally knows how to switch on genes that provide instructions for making liver proteins. And a bone cell knows how to switch genes for liver cell proteins off and how to turn genes for bone cell proteins on. Exactly how cells are able to selectively switch different genes to the ON and OFF positions is one of the great mysteries of nature. If we understood exactly how this happens we would not only understand how diseases like cancer develop, but we would also understand how a fertilized egg gives rise to a complete human being, and how a tiny seed gives rise to a plant with roots and leaves and flowers.

With a requirement for such fine-tuning, you can well imagine that the switches that control the different genes in DNA are elaborate and sensitive, just as they are in any delicate machine. And all elaborate and sensitive processes have the potential for going awry. Among the many different protein machines in cells are some that carry out functions that are specifically required for the cells to grow properly. These machines determine when a cell should divide in two and when it should not. They specify that when a cell is surrounded by other cells it should respect their territory and should not invade their space. If for any reason these protein machines for normal cell growth do not function exactly the way they are supposed to, the growth of cells can become severely deranged. Such cells may now divide and increase in number and may start invading the territory of their neighbors. In other words, *if the particular protein machines that regulate the growth of cells don't work properly, cells can become cancerous.* In Question 12 we'll discuss exactly how and why certain types of proteins become defective or are made at the wrong time or in the wrong amounts.

First, I would like to stress the fundamental importance of appreciating that we are never going to understand how things go wrong in cells and result in diseases like cancer unless we understand how things go *right* in cells and result in normal growth. Cancer research can't simply be confined to the study of cancer cells. Cancer research also requires a detailed understanding of the biology of normal cells. If we didn't know that in normal cells DNA contains genes, and that genes provide the instructions for making protein machines which in turn control the normal growth of cells, we could never hope to comprehend that cancer actually happens when any of these events goes wrong.

The basic rules of nature that govern the way cells work, including the way they grow, are not very different in people and mice and frogs and flies. In fact, if you showed me a single cell under a microscope I couldn't tell you whether it came from a frog or a fly or a person. And because mice and frogs and flies are often much easier to study in the laboratory than cells from people, many important insights that have emerged in cancer research in recent years have come from the study of these simple living forms, from what we call basic biology.

The relationship between the way things work properly and the way they can go wrong is entirely obvious when we think about real machines in our everyday life, such as tractors and cars and TVs. You certainly expect the mechanic who fixes your car to know exactly how cars work, don't you? But somehow when it comes to medical research we forget the critical relationship between basic biology and cancer research. Too often we're reluctant to spend money to find out how mice and frogs and flies work, but at the same time we want to cure cancer. We can't have one without the other.

How do agents
that cause
cancer do their
dirty work?

12

Medicine, to produce health, has to examine disease;
and music, to create harmony,
must investigate discord.

—*Plutarch*

We know that cigarette smoking and prolonged exposure to asbestos have a definite relationship to the incidence of lung cancer, that smoking cigars and pipes increases the risk of cancer of the mouth and throat, and that exposure to large amounts of X-rays increases the risk of leukemia and other types of cancer. How do these carcinogens work? To rephrase this question in the context of the preceding discussion, how do these agents cause the protein machines that determine the normal growth of cells to become defective or to be made at the wrong time or in the wrong amount?

Among the many chemicals in tobacco smoke are some that can alter the DNA (the stuff that genes are made of), and hence the genes themselves. Remember that every time a cell divides it gives rise to two *identical* daughter cells. In order for this to happen an identical copy of the DNA must be made and one copy must be distributed to each of the daughter cells. Indeed, it is precisely the fact that every new cell inherits an identical copy of DNA that provides for each new cell being identical to its parent; that's why DNA is sometimes referred to as the *genetic material* of cells. But if the DNA in a particular cell, for example, a lung cell, is altered by chemicals in tobacco smoke, these alterations will also be copied during the process of duplicating DNA. Because this process is repeated every time a cell divides, all the descendants of that particular cell will inherit altered copies of DNA.

How Do Agents That Cause Cancer Do Their Dirty Work?

The alterations in DNA that are caused by chemicals we inhale, or eat, or drink, or take into our bodies in any other way, are referred to as *DNA damage*, and the alterations that DNA damage causes in genes are called *mutations*. Both chemicals and physical agents (such as X-rays) in the environment that cause mutations in genes are therefore called *mutagens* or *mutagenic agents*. And because many mutagens can cause cells to become cancerous, mutagens and carcinogens are frequently the same thing.

Since mutations alter genes you might suspect that they also alter the instructions that specify the manufacture of particular protein machines, and this is indeed the case. A particular protein may still be made at the correct time and even in the correct amount. But if the gene that specifies this protein is mutated, the protein will be incapable of working correctly or, in some instances, of working at all.

Mutation of genes is a random process. Any of the fifty thousand genes in the DNA of a particular cell can be mutated, and so any of the protein machines that are specified by these thousands of genes can become faulty or defective. Many such problems may be inconsequential for the cell because the affected functions aren't critically important for the health of that cell, or because the cell may have a backup mechanism for that function. But if a particular protein machine normally functions in making sure that cells grow properly, then a defect in that protein can result in that cell becoming cancerous. So carcinogens damage DNA on a random basis and can produce permanent mutations in genes. If by chance these mutated genes specify instructions for proteins that are required for the normal growth of cells, those cells may become cancerous.

The normal growth of cells is not dependent on just one protein machine. Cellular growth is a complicated affair that requires a large number of different proteins, perhaps as many as several hundred. It isn't necessary to knock out the instructions in all of these genes to make a cancer cell. But we now know that in order for a cell to become cancerous the normal function of at least several genes involved in cell growth must be upset, perhaps as many as ten and as few as six genes.

Let's return to the specific example of lung cancer caused by smoking. Imagine that among the billions of cells in the lung one particular cell suffers DNA damage that results in a mutational change in gene A, which instructs the gene in the manufacture of protein A, a protein required for the normal growth of lung cells. A defect in protein A may not affect that particular cell and it will continue to grow and divide normally. But now let's imagine that at some time in the future that same cell, or much more likely one of its many descendants (which of course have all inherited a defective copy of gene A) suffers a second mutational change in a different gene that we'll call gene B, which instructs the gene in the manufacture of protein B, a second protein required for the normal growth of lung cells. The resulting alteration in protein B may still be inconsequential to the growth of the cell. However, all the descendants of this cell will now have mutations in *two* genes which are important for cell growth. If this process continues because of continual DNA damage caused by mutagens in tobacco smoke, eventually the alteration of some critical number of genes, perhaps six or ten of them, will accumulate in one particular cell and that cell will escape the controls of normal growth: it will become cancerous. It will be the first cancer cell in that person's lung and when that cell divides there will be two and then four and then eight cancer cells and so on. *Hence, cancer is thought of as a process that involves multiple independent mutations that alter the function of multiple independent genes, and hence of multiple proteins that provide for the normal growth of cells.*

Despite the fact that the DNA of cells may be frequently exposed to agents that damage DNA, such as the DNA of lung cells in smokers, mutations in genes are actually very rare events. A mutation in any particular gene happens only in about one in one million cells. One of the reasons for this is that cells have the ability to fix a lot of the damage in their DNA before mutations happen. We'll talk more about how cells fix damaged DNA presently.

Because mutations are rather rare and because six to ten particular genes among the fifty thousand genes in a cell must be affected to result in cancerous changes, you can readily appreciate why it takes so long for cancer to develop, hence why it is usually a disease of older people. This is particularly well documented for lung cancer associated with cigarette smoking. The incidence of lung cancer began to increase sharply in men about 1940 and in women about 1960. Cigarette smoking became a widespread habit in men around 1920, but it took twenty years for this behavior to be reflected in the incidence of lung cancer. Similarly, cigarette smoking among women only became really popular and acceptable during World War II, so once again we see about a twenty-year lag before lung cancer incidence began to climb.

You can now also understand why the more one smokes and the longer one smokes, the greater is the chance that at some point a single cell (or one of it's descendants) in one's lungs is going to accumulate defects in genes A, B, C, D, E, and F. This is fundamentally what the *risk factor* that we keep referring to is all about. The risk is essentially the chance that one particular cell (or its relatively small number of descendants) in the body will sustain mutations in a particular set of genes.

The factor of risk is actually more complicated than this because the chance of getting a "hit," a mutation, in a particular set of genes is not totally random for any person. Not everyone who smokes, even heavily, gets lung cancer. In fact, as I indicated earlier, nine out of ten smokers don't get lung cancer. Why not? Each of us is a unique individual and functions a little differently. Some of us are at an increased risk of cancer because we are born with defective genes that are important for controlling the growth of cells. We'll discuss the importance of genetic risk for cancer in Question 16. But additionally, some of us have a better chance than others to prevent mutations from occurring in genes. In the answer to the next question you'll discover that we are not totally defenseless against the damaging effects of carcinogens. For example, our cells can fix some of the damage that happens in our DNA. But for reasons that we don't yet understand, some of us fix DNA better than others. Some of us are blessed with protein machines for fixing DNA with engines like a BMW's; others of us have machines with engines like a model-T Ford's! Obviously the better your cells are at fixing DNA, the less risk they have for cancer. But don't feel you can push your luck too far—risk factors can be dangerous!

As a corollary to increasing risk for cancer we can also decrease the risk. Giving up smoking certainly reduces one's risk of lung cancer. If lung cancer develops only when a lung cell has accumulated mutational alterations in genes A, B, C, D, E, and F, then quite obviously if one quits smoking when the most severely affected lung cell has mutations in just genes A, B, and C, one will reduce the future risk of that cell also accumulating mutations in genes D, E, and F.

So much for how chemical and physical agents in the real world cause cancer. However, recall my suggestion that in the complete absence of exposure to any environmental agents cancer would probably still be a relatively common disease. Why? The unfortunate fact is that alterations in genes can happen naturally. As one example of how "natural" damage occurs in DNA, remember that our cells naturally make many chemicals that can also damage DNA. As is the case with mutagens and carcinogens present in plants and vegetables, we have to accept this as an unfortunate consequence of some other useful process in life. The simple fact is that some of the by-products—the waste disposal if you will—of some of the factories in our cells are toxic and can damage our own DNA.

As a second example of "natural" DNA damage let's reconsider the process of duplicating DNA every time a cell divides. The instructional property of genes that determines which particular protein machines are made by each cell is stored in the DNA as a shorthand code that cells know how to decipher. This code, which translates information stored in DNA into proteins, is called the *genetic code*. It is the code whereby the master molecule, DNA, unfolds its blueprint for life. Because the genetic code is so fundamental to life, biologists often write and speak of it in highly reverent terms. So that's what all the fuss is about.

In order for every cell to function in exactly the same way as its parent it is clearly very important that the code not be altered from one generation of cells to the next. It is crucial that the process of copying DNA be extremely accurate every time a cell divides. In fact, the process of duplicating DNA is so good that the genes in most of our cells change very, very infrequently. But every now and again a mistake is made, which can result in mutations without any assistance from synthetic chemical carcinogens and mutagens in the environment. When genes that are crucial for the normal growth of cells are altered by these natural accidents these events can lead to cancerous change in cells in exactly the same way as the mutations caused by environmental agents.

Incorrect copying of DNA is just one way of generating mutations in genes naturally. There are other ways by which this can happen. DNA is after all a chemical compound, and because all chemical compounds are inherently unstable to varying extents, DNA can and does change its chemistry quite spontaneously. Fortunately, as is the case with the inaccurate copying of DNA, this happens very rarely, but when it does, a mutation in a gene can be generated. So there are many ways by which mutations can arise in genes. And that is why one can get lung cancer even if one does not smoke.

Before ending this brief discussion of DNA and genes and proteins, I would like to explain why the genetic code is often spoken of by scientists in such reverent terms and why we worship this particular aspect of cell biology so profoundly. Understanding the genetic code and how it is deciphered in cells ranks in scientific importance with understanding gravity, or how the solar system works. It really is that fundamental. And we especially revere this achievement because it happened in our own lifetime, during the past twenty to thirty years. In fact many of the principal scientists involved—the Newtons and Copernicuses of modern biology—are still practicing science today. So we are truly living in very historic times.

The fundamental impetus for this startling achievement came from a discovery made in the mid-1950s by James Watson and Francis Crick, two names that are legendary in science. Watson recounted the events of this scientific breakthrough in a book called *The Double Helix,* which you really should read if you have not already done so. It is eminently readable because, after all, the recounting of a scientific discovery is much like a detective story, and who can resist a good whodunit?

The discovery of the structure of DNA marked the dawn of what is now widely acknowledged as a golden age in the history of science. The ability to understand how cells function at a level as fundamental as decoding instructions in genes has spawned a new type of biology, called *molecular biology.* Less than forty years after the discovery of the structure of DNA, the applications of molecular biology to human disease in general, and cancer in particular, are nothing less than astounding. This is the future of cancer research—the silver lining to the cloud of cancer—and you should know that this future is very bright indeed.

How quickly does a cancer grow?

13

Ever forward, but slowly.
—*Gebhard Leberecht von Blücher*

If you have had the unfortunate experience of accidentally discovering a lump somewhere that turned out to be cancer, you may well have asked yourself the question, How long have I had this? We don't really know how rapidly cancers grow. Most people imagine that a lump is something that emerges over a matter of weeks or months. Not so. There is evidence that it takes longer for cancer to grow than most people realize, probably years in some types of cancer.

In order for a cancer to reach a size where there is a reasonable chance that it can be detected by physical examination or even by using quite sophisticated diagnostic tests it must be about half an inch in diameter. A cancer of such a size actually consists of about a billion cells. Even if we assume that cancers grow exponentially—by the relentless process of every cancer cell doubling every time it divides, which, as I showed you earlier (see the table on page 5), can result in a rapid increase in numbers—it takes many cycles of cell division before we get to a billion.

But when we talk about the growth of cancers we don't consider only the increase in the number of cells. We know that beginning with the very first cell, or with just a few cells, cancers undergo many changes before they become full blown. These changes include the ability to sustain themselves with a proper supply of nutrients, the ability to invade the surrounding cells, and the ability to spread to other parts of the body. These and many other changes in the behavior of the cancer are called *tumor progression*, the progressive evolution of the cancer from one single cell to a full-blown disease. It is this process of tumor progression that takes quite a long time.

Let's consider some well-studied examples that indicate this relative slowness. We have already discussed the fact that the prostate gland is a rather frequent place for cancer to develop. Based on many years of careful record keeping, we know that approximately two out of every thousand men in the United States who are seventy or older are diagnosed with this disease each year. In other words, the annual incidence of cancer of the prostate in men over seventy is about 0.2 percent. Now most hospitals, particularly those associated with medical schools where students, interns, and residents are trained for careers in medicine, carry out as many autopsies as possible in the interests of maintaining high standards of medical practice. An *autopsy* is a procedure carried out after death, during which every organ and tissue in the body is carefully examined for evidence of any disease. (This is indeed how many pathologists spend the rest of their time when they are not interpreting biopsies.) The autopsy provides the ultimate verification of diagnoses made during life. It affords a unique opportunity to discover all sorts of incidental diseases that neither patient nor doctor may even have known about because they were at a very early stage and weren't causing any noticeable discomfort.

Careful examination of the prostate gland during autopsies on men who were seventy or older at the time of death and who died for reasons that had nothing to do with prostate disease has shown that cancers (usually very small) are present in as many as 20 percent of them. Since the incidence of cancer of the prostate diagnosed during life is only 0.2 percent, this means that the actual incidence of prostate cancer is really one hundred times greater than the cases that we know about. Why this hundred-fold discrepancy? One explanation is that cancer of the prostate grows so slowly that it only becomes noticeable in about one in every hundred men with prostate cancer before they die for some other reason.

Let's consider another situation that suggests that many cancers grow rather slowly. A very common form of cancer in women develops in a part of the womb called the *cervix,* which forms the entrance of the womb or *uterus.* As those of you who are mothers well know, the cervix expands greatly during childbirth to allow the baby to pass out of the womb. Epithelial cells in the lining of the cervix become cancerous rather frequently. Because cancer of the cervix is so common and because the cervix is very accessible to examination by doctors, for many years women have been encouraged to have frequent special examinations during which cells from the cervix can be evaluated for cancer using a very simple test called a *Pap smear.* During a Pap smear the cervix is lightly scraped to remove some cells, which are then smeared onto a glass slide, which is examined under the microscope, just like a biopsy. This simple test is named after its inventor, Dr. George Papanicolaou. We'll talk about the Pap smear again in the next question and stress its great importance not only in detecting early cancer of the cervix, but also early changes in cervical cells which can warn us that cancer might soon develop in them.

Such evaluations performed over many years in many thousands of women have led to the discovery that very early cancer of the cervix, at a stage before any cancer cells have invaded the surrounding tissues, occurs most frequently in women who are about thirty-five to forty-five years old. On the other hand, cancer of the cervix that has already invaded the surrounding tissues by the time it is first diagnosed occurs most frequently in women aged about forty-five to fifty-five. A possible explanation for this age difference is that it takes about ten years for the noninvasive form of cancer of the cervix to become the invasive form, suggesting once again that cancer grows rather slowly.

So the conclusion that we can draw from the study of both cancer of the prostate and cancer of the cervix is that even though most cancers of all types are discovered in people over the age of fifty-five, it is likely that the tumor actually started years earlier. The tragedy is that we do not have very effective ways of detecting and hence diagnosing the presence of cancer when it is in its very early stages. We'll come back to this important problem of cancer diagnosis later in the book.

As a cancer grows, it advances through the multiple steps of tumor progression. It starts with a single cancer cell, growing into many thousands of cancer cells, then invading the immediate surroundings, and eventually spreading to other parts of the body. As it grows, its ability to interfere with the health of the patient increases in inverse proportion to its ability to be cured by treatment. Naturally, we would like to know as much as possible about how far every cancer has progressed because it affects the patient's likelihood of surviving cancer. As discussed earlier, when an initial diagnosis of cancer is made, the pathologist who examines the cancer then attempts to determine the state of the cancer growth by *grading* and *staging*. Both the grade of cancer and the stage of cancer are indications of how rapidly and how aggressively the tumor is growing.

When cancer cells are examined under the microscope they look different from normal cells. But the extent to which they look different varies from one cancer to another, and indeed from one part of the cancer to another. In general, the more the cancer cells resemble the normal cells from which they arose the less aggressively the cancer is growing. Based on this criterion—how similar to normal cells cancer cells look—pathologists grade them into four degrees of severity called grades 1, 2, 3, and 4. Grade 1 cancers are considered to be the least aggressive, grade 4 cancers the most aggressive.

In many cases the grade of a cancer is not a particularly reliable indicator of how rapidly and aggressively it will grow. In other words many grade 4 cancers still respond well to treatment and don't grow noticeably faster than grade 1 cancers. Cancer of the prostate in men is a rather notable exception. In general, the worse the grade of prostatic cancer, the worse the prognosis.

Much more important from the point of view of the outlook for successful treatment is the *stage* of the cancer. Criteria for staging cancer that can be employed uniformly around the world have been agreed on by two different cancer agencies. The Union Internationale Contre Cancer (IUCC), an international agency, uses three primary criteria for staging. These are the size of the cancer, spread to neighboring lymph nodes, and metastasis to other sites in the body. Each of these criteria is given a numerical value that varies somewhat for each type of cancer according to defined standards of evaluation. The total numerical score provides a staging number for that particular cancer. The American Joint Committee on Cancer Staging uses a slightly different variation that includes a staging rank of 0, 1, 2, 3, and 4.

Let's consider the way in which several of the most common cancers are staged. According to the criteria set forth by the Joint Committee on Cancer Staging, *cancer of the breast* is staged as follows:

Stage 1   A cancer that measures less than two inches in diameter with no spread to lymph nodes or to distant parts of the body.

Stage 2   A cancer that measures less than two inches in diameter with spread to lymph nodes but not to distant parts of the body.

Stage 3   A cancer of any size with spread to the skin of the breast, or to the muscles of the chest or the chest wall and involvement of lymph nodes, but no spread to distant sites.

Stage 4   Any cancer that has spread to distant parts of the body.

A method frequently used for staging *cancer of the large bowel (colon)* uses a set of criteria called the Dukes classification, which not only evaluates whether the cancer has spread to lymph nodes and to distant sites, but also exactly how deeply it has penetrated into the wall of the intestine.

Stage A   A cancer that is limited to the very surface lining of the colon.

Stage B1   A cancer that has invaded deeper into the wall of the colon, but with no lymph node involvement.

Stage B2   A cancer that has invaded through the entire wall of the colon, but with no lymph node involvement.

Stage C1   A cancer that has not yet invaded through the entire wall of the colon, but which has already spread to neighboring lymph nodes.

Stage C2   A cancer that has infiltrated through the entire wall of the colon, and which has also spread to neighboring lymph nodes.

Stage D   A cancer that has spread to distant sites of the body.

Cancer of the prostate is staged differently by different oncologists. One method often used is the following:

Stage A   A cancer that is discovered accidentally after removal of the prostate for what was thought to be a benign condition.

Stage B   A cancer that can be felt by the examining doctor during a rectal examination, but which appears to be confined to the prostate gland.

Stage C   A cancer that has spread beyond the prostate to neighboring tissues, but which has not spread to distant sites of the body.

Stage D   A cancer that has spread to distant sites of the body.

Slightly different criteria are applied for the staging of other types of cancer but they fundamentally all take into account a very commonsense and rational way of assigning a score to the cancer based on how rapidly the cancer has grown and how far it has progressed.

Can I catch cancer from someone?

14

*We are often more frightened than hurt:
our troubles spring more often
from fancy than reality.*

—Seneca

The great majority of cancers are not caused by any sort of infectious agent, so there's nothing to catch. However, in recent years we have come to appreciate the fact that certain cancers are clearly related to certain viruses. Let's consider the virus that has been most widely talked and written about as far as human cancer is concerned: the *AIDS* virus. This disease—*a*cquired *i*mmune *d*eficiency *s*yndrome—which is taking such a terrible toll on human health and life all over the world, is indeed caused by a virus. The virus itself is actually called *HIV* (for *h*uman *i*mmunodeficiency *v*irus). The disease AIDS is not cancer itself; it is a disease that is frequently *associated* with cancer. However, when cancer occurs in people with AIDS the virus does not cause the cancer directly; the relationship between the virus and the cancer, which we'll talk about in more detail later, is indirect.

Regardless of exactly how the AIDS virus results in the development of cancer, it is certainly true that if one is infected with this virus one has a significantly increased risk of getting cancer. But unlike the virus that causes the common cold or flu or chicken pox or measles, it is not easy to "catch" the AIDS virus. As you probably know, one way that the virus can be communicated is by sexual contact. Pregnant women who are HIV-positive can communicate the virus to their offspring during childbirth, by breast feeding, and possibly during pregnancy itself. Outside of these situations the only way there is any significant risk of becoming infected is if the virus is directly introduced into your blood, for example, during a blood transfusion. The reason for this is that the AIDS virus can only live in certain cells of the body, cells that are extremely difficult for it to find unless the virus is in the bloodstream. In fact, outside of sexual contact, transfusions with blood taken from someone with AIDS, and intravenous drug use, the only situations in which this has happened are extremely rare ones in which people, usually health professionals, have accidentally had blood from AIDS patients introduced directly into their own bloodstream. So you cannot catch AIDS by being in the same room as an AIDS patient, or by any other form of normal social interaction. The virus for the common cold or flu or other viruses are much more contagious because these viruses can live and grow in cells in the nose, throat, or lungs.

In addition to AIDS, certain other viruses are associated with particular cancers. There is evidence that many cases of cancer of the cervix in women are caused by the *papillomavirus*, which can be transmitted by heterosexual activity. The virus can also cause completely benign warts of the genitals in both men and women, but does not seem to be associated with genital cancer in men. Herein lies the importance of the Pap smear that we talked about earlier. Long before cells in the cervix become cancerous they undergo a *premalignant change*, a change that is not yet cancer, but a warning sign that cancer may develop. A Pap smear detects these premalignant changes, and when they are identified the abnormal cells in the cervix can be removed by simple treatments. While there is certainly every reason to be careful about sexual transmission of the papillomavirus, the important point is that regular Pap smears are a much more effective way of preventing cancer of the cervix. Every woman should have such a test once a year.

Do I have
natural defenses
against cancer?

15

Thousands upon thousands of persons
have studied disease. Almost no one
has studied health.

—*Adelle Davis*

You will surely be pleased to know that we are not totally defenseless against the various forces that produce cancerous changes in individual cells and that allow very tiny cancers to persist and grow in the body. First, let's discuss some of the defenses against the mutational changes in genes which can alter the function of the protein machines that are so important for the normal growth of cells.

Since the dawn of evolution cells have been exposed to environmental agents that can cause DNA damage, or harm to the instructional units of DNA, the coding units. For example, even though sunlight is an indispensable source of energy on our planet, the sun puts out ultraviolet rays that are very harmful to DNA. You can well appreciate how much of a problem this presented to the earliest life-forms on our planet. Since the DNA of these primitive organisms was constantly bombarded with ultraviolet rays, they would have rapidly accumulated mutational alterations in their genes, many of the protein machines that carry out vital cellular functions would have been wrecked, and their cells simply would not have been able to function, unless the damage to their DNA was handled in some special way. Many millions of years ago this problem was solved by the evolution of mechanisms for fixing damaged DNA. We call the work of these mechanisms *DNA repair*.

In addition to ultraviolet radiation from the sun, the earliest life-forms also had to cope with other naturally occurring sources of damage from the environment. Astronauts have to be carefully protected from X-rays (cosmic rays), which are present in space in very high amounts. This type of radiation is also emitted on the earth, although in much smaller amounts, by naturally radioactive compounds. Such radiations are also potentially damaging to the DNA in cells. In a conventional X-ray only tiny amounts of radiation enter one's body and cells are able to repair the resulting DNA damage. Cells have even learned how to recognize and correct some of the very rare mistakes that happen spontaneously during the process of copying the informational units in DNA in order to duplicate DNA before cells divide, and they can also repair the natural damage that arises from the inherent instability of DNA as a chemical.

So in fact, after millions of years of evolution human cells have acquired a pretty effective repertoire of DNA repair mechanisms. Obviously these repair mechanisms were not specifically designed for protection against synthetic industrial chemicals which cells have never encountered in nature. But, luckily, the same repair mechanisms that work on damage caused by sunlight and X-rays also happen to work on DNA damage caused by the carcinogenic compounds in tobacco smoke and many other types of synthetic carcinogens.

Well then, if our cells are smart enough to fix DNA damage, why do we get mutations? Like all machines, the capacity of cells to fix damaged DNA is limited. And in the face of continued exposure the DNA of cells eventually suffers permanent alterations. It would seem logical that if we could somehow improve the ability of our cells to repair damaged DNA we might be able to prevent some of the earliest changes in cells that can result in their becoming cancerous. We don't know how to do this yet. But this experimental approach to combating cancer is an important one that will certainly evolve in future years.

DNA repair is a defense against cancer that operates to *prevent* the changes in cells that can result in their becoming cancerous. But we also know that once cancer cells have actually arisen in the body they can sometimes be eliminated by natural processes—by a second line of defense, so to speak. How does this happen?

All of the cells in your body are very personally yours, in the sense that when cells from another person or another organism are presented to your body they are instantly recognized as not belonging to you and are rejected. The recognition and rejection of foreign cells is carried out by a special system called the *immune system*. It treats cells that are not from your body as if they were foreign invaders that do not belong and kills them. That's how you recover from any type of infection, including something as trivial as a cold. Your immune system actually hunts down the invading bacteria or viruses, recognizes them as foreign to your body, and disposes of them.

Sometimes this powerful system can be a disadvantage. For example, this special ability to tell the difference between cells that are uniquely yours and cells that are not yours also triggers the killing (*rejection*) of transplanted organs and tissues, such as hearts and kidneys and even skin, in people who need new organs. As soon as the new organs are introduced into the body the immune system recognizes them as foreign intruders and kills them. A little later we'll address this problem of rejection with respect to the treatment of cancer by the transplantation of bone marrow cells.

What does the immune system have to do with cancer? Well, cancer cells not only behave differently from normal cells in terms of their growth and their ability to invade the body, they also often change in ways that make them appear different or foreign to the immune system. When this happens the cancer cells are hunted down and destroyed. We call this process of seeking and destroying cells *immune surveillance*. As is true of DNA repair, this ability of the immune system to kill cancer cells is limited and eventually some of the cells escape this defense mechanism. But there is evidence that very small cancers in the body may be completely cured in this way, so that we never really know that we had them. You may have heard or read about cases in which a cancer, sometimes even one that had spread quite widely, suddenly disappeared from a person's body, never to return. This happens very rarely, but it does happen. It is probable that in these mysterious cases some kind of signal suddenly triggered the immune system to totally eradicate the cancer. We don't know how this happens and why it doesn't always eliminate all cancer cells as soon as they arise. If we did we would have a very powerful way of treating cancer. Cancer researchers are trying very hard to take advantage of this ability of the immune system to kill cancer cells, and we'll discuss it again when we talk about the treatment of cancer in Question 18.

This is an opportune time to discuss the other side of the coin with respect to the immune system. What happens if the immune system is not working properly? You might expect that if the immune system is depressed for any reason, the ability to eradicate cancer cells might be compromised and the risk of developing a full-blown cancer would be increased. This is indeed the case and nowhere is this more dramatically demonstrated than in AIDS (acquired immune deficiency syndrome), the viral disease discussed briefly earlier. This name was given to the disease because the virus causes a progressive deterioration or deficiency of the immune system. "Acquired" is used to distinguish this type of immune deficiency from those one can be born with, as a genetic or inherited disease, and "syndrome" is simply another word for disease.

The AIDS virus attacks, multiplies in, and kills the very cells in the immune system that provide protection against infections and that hunt and destroy foreign cells, including cancer cells which the immune system no longer recognizes as its own "self." Eventually the loss of these AIDS-destroyed cells becomes so severe that patients with AIDS show evidence of cancers that they might otherwise not have known about. So the AIDS virus does not directly cause cancer; it predisposes to cancer by destroying an extremely important protective mechanism, the ability of the immune system to kill cancer cells very soon after they develop. The fact that many AIDS victims actually do develop some form of cancer indicates just how critical this protective mechanism of immune surveillance is. Incidentally, cancer is not the only disease to which people with AIDS are predisposed. Because the immune system is compromised, these individuals are also highly susceptible to a variety of infectious diseases.

From this discussion you might deduce that if your ability to repair DNA damage is impaired in some way you also might have an increased risk of getting cancer. This is so. We have already talked about the fact that some people apparently fix DNA better than others, but in the extreme case some can actually be born with a severely reduced ability to carry out DNA repair. Such people have a profoundly increased risk of various sorts of cancers. One of the most dramatic examples we know of is a disease called *xeroderma* (pronounced zeroderma) *pigmentosum*, XP for short. Fortunately, this is an extremely rare genetic disease. Only about one in 200,000 people in the United States, the United Kingdom, and Europe suffer from it. People who have this inherited disease are extremely sensitive to sunlight and have an extremely high probability of developing a variety of skin cancers. The study of XP and the discovery that it results from defective DNA repair not only indicates the important role of DNA damage in causing cancer, but also provides evidence that ultraviolet radiation from the sun is a very potent carcinogen. You will recall that each year something like 700,000 new cases of skin cancer are diagnosed, so be careful how you enjoy the sun!

In addition to DNA repair and immune surveillance, there are other ways in which the body is protected from cancer to some extent, but we understand these less well. Let's return to the question of DNA damage. Many of the chemicals that can cause genes to become altered, and which therefore have the potential for causing mutations, can be destroyed or neutralized in the body. Some of our cells have specialized protein machines that alter these compounds so as to render them innocuous or to facilitate their rapid removal from the body. Once again, with this process, it is very likely that there is individual variation in the population. If you are relatively inefficient in these neutralizing reactions you might be at a greater risk for damaging your DNA. Conversely, if you have a superefficient neutralizing system you probably reduce your risk of damaging your DNA. So here is another possible reason for the fact that not everyone who smokes gets cancer.

In addition to the ability to repair damaged genes, seek out and destroy cancer cells, and neutralize some chemicals that have the potential for causing cancer, our bodies may have other, not yet discovered, natural defenses against cancer. It would be nice to know about them, wouldn't it? One way of trying to identify such natural defenses is to study people who have a genetic predisposition to cancer, in other words, people who are born with a defect in some function that normally protects against the development of cancer. Just as is the case with the genetic disease XP discussed earlier, in which a reduced ability to repair damaged DNA predisposes to skin cancer, so we would expect that individuals with some other genetic predisposition to cancer may be defective in some other natural defense mechanism. A good way of identifying such people is to search for families in which the incidence of cancer is much higher than expected in the general population. But the identification of families with a clear-cut genetic predisposition to cancer is also not easy. Remember that we are dealing with a group of diseases that affects one in every three people in the population. With such a high incidence, the chances that more than one member of the same family will get cancer by sheer bad luck is also very high. In the next question we'll examine true genetic predisposition to cancer and the profound impact that this topic has had on our understanding of the disease.

Can one be born with an increased risk of getting cancer?

16

We come into the world with the mark
of our descent. . .
—*Alain Rene Lesage*

Yes, one can. We have already discussed a particular example of this—a predisposition to skin cancer due to the reduced ability to repair damaged DNA, as is the case with people who are born with the disease xeroderma pigmentosum, characterized by mutations in the genes that specify the manufacture of proteins for fixing damaged DNA. So xeroderma pigmentosum sufferers have defective DNA repair machines; as a consequence they sustain a much larger amount of DNA damage in the cells of their skin when they are exposed to sunlight.

Aside from such defective genes, one can be born with defects in other genes which also increase the likelihood that one will get cancer. Let's revisit the concept that the normal growth of cells is determined by multiple genes that provide the instructions for multiple proteins. We discussed the notion that mutations in anywhere from six to ten of these particular genes in any one cell may be sufficient to make that cell cancerous, and that these mutations can accumulate over many years because of natural damage to DNA, or damage caused by agents in our environment. These genes normally function to help cells grow properly, so if we wanted to give them a name it would be reasonable to call them "cell-growth genes" or something similar. But in view of the fact that these genes cause cells to become cancerous when they *don't* work properly, we're going to refer to them as "cancer genes."

Up to this point we've been considering genes that are defective because of mutations in cells such as lung cells. Since mutations represent permanent alterations in genes, they are of course passed on to all the descendants of that particular cell in the lung. Mutations in a lung cell or a breast cell cannot be passed on to one's children, however. But remember that every cell in the body contains the same amount of DNA and the same number of genes. So just as one can develop a mutation in a "cancer gene" in a lung cell, one can also develop a mutation in a "cancer gene" in any other cell in the body, including sperm cells and egg cells. If that particular sperm cell or egg cell gives rise to an embryo, every cell in the baby's body will carry this mutation because the mutation was inherited from one single cell at the moment of conception. In other words, one can be born with a "cancer gene" that is mutated at the outset of life.

If a particular type of cell—a lung cell for example—becomes cancerous only after ten "cancer genes" are affected by mutations, then even if you are born with one defective gene it will not make a big difference in your chances of getting lung cancer. Even though every cell in your lungs carries one mutated "cancer gene" from the time of birth, any single lung cell must still accumulate the other nine mutations independently. Now you can understand why for most types of cancer it is extremely difficult to determine whether or not there really is a genetic predisposition.

But if it only takes mutations in two "cancer genes" to give rise to a particular type of cancer, then if you are born with one of these two genes already defective, it obviously only takes one more mutation to result in your getting lung cancer. In this case the genetic predisposition to this type of cancer will be much more evident. Furthermore, as you might expect if only one gene needs to be altered by a mutation after birth, this cancer will have a high chance of developing at an early age. This is precisely what happens with a particular type of cancer called *retinoblastoma*, which develops in cells in the retina of the eye. Some children are born with a defective "cancer gene" which they inherited from their parents. Even though they carry this mutated gene in every cell in their body, this particular "cancer gene" predisposes them uniquely to retinoblastoma. If they then acquire a mutation in a second "cancer gene" in cells of the retina, because of some type of DNA damage in these cells during life, they will develop this type of cancer, frequently at a rather early age. Fortunately, retinoblastoma is a tumor that can be very effectively treated when diagnosed early.

To consider another example of genetic predisposition to cancer, let's revisit the problem of polyps of the intestine, which we discussed in Question 6 as examples of benign tumors that can sometimes become malignant. Some people are born with a disease called *hereditary multiple polyposis* in which they have many hundreds, sometimes even thousands of these intestinal polyps, and they have a much higher chance of getting cancer of the colon than people who don't have this disease. We now know that the reason for this increased risk of colon cancer is that in addition to being born with many intestinal polyps, these people also inherit a "cancer gene," a defective gene which in normal people helps prevent cancerous changes from occurring in these polyps of the colon. So once again the dice are loaded from the time of birth.

As I indicated earlier, an important clue that someone might have a hereditary predisposition to cancer is the presence of a particular type of cancer in that person's family at a higher frequency than that expected in the general population. Remember that this can be tricky because cancer is such a common disease in general. Another clue is the occurrence of cancer at an early age, as is often the case with retinoblastoma, for example. Recently a "cancer gene" was discovered that results in an increased risk of breast cancer in women, suggesting that at least for some people breast cancer may have a genetic component.

The ability to identify genes that predispose to cancer in the population is a very exciting and very recent advance. Cancer researchers call these "cancer genes" *oncogenes* (from the Greek *onkos*, meaning "mass" or "bulk," which also gives us *oncology*, the whole science or field of tumors—that is, cancer). The reason for all the excitement is that once scientists have determined that a particular gene is present in the cells of any living organism, including the human organism, that gene can often be isolated as a tiny bit of DNA and millions of copies of it can be made in the laboratory. The technology of isolating genes from cells and making multiple identical copies of them is called *gene cloning*. In addition, once genes have been isolated and cloned, scientists can read the coded instructions for manufacturing the particular protein which is specified by that gene, just as the cell can. Armed with this information, researchers can sometimes even deduce that protein machine's function in the cell. And all this without having to study the protein itself. That's something like reading the ingredients list of a recipe and knowing exactly what the dish will taste like before one prepares it!

Once we know exactly what a particular protein machine does and how it works in causing cancerous changes in cells, we have the potential for interfering with that protein. In other words, we have an opportunity for designing novel treatments or prevention strategies for cancer based on disrupting or eliminating whatever it is that particular protein does in cells to produce cancer. In time we might even be able to replace that oncogene with a perfectly healthy version of the cloned gene. These general strategies represent the exciting future of cancer treatment.

The isolation of oncogenes offers a second important dividend. Even though scientists are able to isolate individual genes from cells, the process of cloning a gene requires a lot of hard work and is very time consuming. But once a gene has been cloned from a particular cell it is rather easy to isolate that same gene from any other cell. So whenever a particular oncogene is cloned it is feasible to think about screening entire populations to find out how many people have such a "cancer gene" in their cells. Returning to the concept of genes A, B, C, D, and so on, all of which must be injured or mutated in any one cell for cancer to develop, the availability of these as cloned genes will make it possible to find out if a person was born with an already compromised gene and therefore have a genetic predisposition to certain types of cancers.

This type of research is so new that scientists are still debating ethical questions concerning the use of such information. The moral dilemma is straightforward. Would you like to be told that you were born with an increased risk for a particular type of cancer if nothing in the way of useful intervention can yet be practiced, especially if that predisposition does not necessarily mean that you will get cancer? I leave you to come to your own decision about this question.

You should recognize that the issue of predisposition to cancer is complicated and doesn't only reside in the genes you were born with. There are indications that for many cancers factors such as hormonal balance and other physiological parameters are important determinants for risk. This has become well appreciated for breast cancer in women. Aside from age and family history, which strongly suggest the operation of genetic factors, the risk of breast cancer in women is also influenced by the age at which menstruation started and their age when their first baby was born. The earlier the age of first menstruation, the greater the risk of cancer. And women who have their first child later in life are at an increased risk for breast cancer compared to women who have their first child earlier. This relationship to childbirth is especially interesting because the correlation is not with the first pregnancy and does not include miscarriages or abortions. It is specifically related to the first live birth.

How can I reduce my risk of cancer?

17

*Your prayer must be for a sound mind
in a sound body.*

—*Juvenal*

Earlier I tried to convince you that, in general, chemical and physical agents in the environment are not major contributors to the incidence of cancer in most parts of the world. We do not live in a veritable sea of carcinogens produced by industrial pollution. But that is not to say that the environment and our lifestyles do not influence our risk of various cancers to some extent. They most certainly do and you most certainly can reduce your cancer risk by how and where you work and live.

Let's very briefly consider the workplace. The observations of Sir Percival Pott, the English surgeon who first noted the correlation between chimney sweeping and cancer of the scrotum nearly two hundred years ago, marked the beginning of the formal science of *occupational carcinogenesis*, the study of the relationship between cancer risk and the type of work one does. We now know that occupational exposure to many chemicals and mixtures of chemicals such as benzene, chromium, tar, and nickel, to mention a few, and to physical agents such as ionizing radiation (X-rays) and asbestos fibers, pose definite cancer risks. Based on the unfortunate experiences of the past, much stricter regulations governing the safety of the workplace are in effect in most Westernized countries. In the United States, the Occupational Safety and Health Administration (OSHA) is empowered to regulate such matters.

Agents that pose a cancer hazard in the workplace are generally quite easily identified because many employees are likely to be affected, and so their occupation can be identified as a common denominator. Identifying carcinogens in the home and in our general lifestyles is more of a problem because there are so many different variables to check out. Every now and then the media report the occurrence of so-called cancer clusters, suggesting that the incidence of cancer in some town or county is higher than expected and raising fears that the community is being exposed to some unidentified carcinogen. These instances of cancer clusters can be difficult to evaluate. Just as in the case of families, the occurrence of what appear to be unexpectedly large numbers of cancer cases in limited geographic areas may reflect nothing more than pure chance. In this regard it is worth noting that when a particular environmental carcinogen is indeed operating in a limited geographic situation, it is typical to find an increase in a particular type of cancer rather than many types of different cancers.

There are compelling indications that different lifestyles do pose different risks for cancer. The frequency with which this happens varies in different countries and in different races. For example, if we return to the records on cancer deaths in different parts of the world during the three-year period 1984 to 1986, we find that in Switzerland slightly more than 33 men per 100,000 died of prostatic cancer, compared with about 23 men per 100,000 in the United States. However, in Japan only about 5 men per 100,000 died of this disease. But when Japanese men immigrate to the United States their incidence of prostatic cancer rises. The immediate question that comes to mind when one encounters such a startling difference is whether it reflects differences that are racial (genetic) or environmental (lifestyle). A very strong indication that environmental influences are at work in prostatic cancer is the observation that when Japanese men move to Western countries such as the United States, the incidence of cancer of the prostate goes up. This suggests that the low incidence of this type of cancer in Japanese men is not due simply to racial (genetic) differences between Japanese and Caucasian men. Rather, it suggests that Japan represents a relatively low-risk environment for prostatic cancer, whereas the United States represents a high risk environment. Exactly what factor or factors in these environments are important is not known.

Other epidemiological data about cancer point a finger at the environment and lifestyle. If we compare the lowest incidence in the world of certain types of cancers to the highest incidence of the same cancers, we find that cancer of the skin is more than two hundred times as common in Queensland, Australia than in Bombay, India. This reflects the different levels of ultraviolet radiation from the sun that penetrate through the ozone layer in these two parts of the world, and the protection that having a dark skin affords against skin cancer caused by sunlight. Cancer of the esophagus is three hundred times more common in northeast Iran than in Nigeria. Genetic factors may be partly responsible for this, but more likely, people in northeast Iran are eating something that people in Nigeria are not.

Even within a single country, such as the United States, the cancer death rates differ from one state to another. The total death rate for all types of cancer is highest in New York, Connecticut, Rhode Island, and Massachusetts, and is lowest in Idaho, Wyoming, and Utah. We don't know why this is but it can't be genetic, because the people living in the northeastern United States and in the mountain states are not racially different. So these differences presumably reflect subtle but important variations in lifestyle and environment in these parts of the country. We certainly all know that it's more stressful trying to find a taxicab in New York city than in Boise, Idaho!

Can agents in the environment that cause cancer be detected? Yes, chemicals can be tested and many of them can be identified as villains. Testing the environment for chemicals that can cause cancer is an important way both of identifying carcinogens and protecting the public from unnecessary and excessive exposure. There are many ways of carrying out such tests. Naturally, they are done on animals, with the reasonable assumption that if a substance is carcinogenic for mice or guinea pigs it is likely to be carcinogenic for humans.

You should recognize that there are some problems with the tests that directly test chemicals in animals. They are very time-consuming because just as cancer takes a long time to develop in people, so it does in animals. Large numbers of animals must be used to make the tests valid, so it is very expensive to use this type of test on a routine basis. A chemical that causes cancer in animals such as rats or mice may not cause cancer in different animals such as guinea pigs. If a test is negative it may mean that it was really tested on the wrong animal. Finally, the way in which many animal tests are performed has generated controversy about their interpretation, and not every expert in the field agrees that they are reliable indicators of the likelihood that a given chemical can cause cancer in people.

Remember that carcinogenic chemicals in our environment are thought to act by damaging the DNA in our cells, resulting in permanent changes or mutations in our genes. So an indirect way of testing substances for their likelihood of causing cancer is to ask whether these substances do indeed cause mutations in genes. Such tests don't require live animals; they can be done with individual cells in the laboratory. Since genes in the cells of mice and frogs and even bacteria react with chemical substances in pretty much the same way as do genes from people, it really doesn't make a big difference which cells are used to test the effect of chemicals on genes. This has facilitated the development of relatively quick and simple tests to screen many chemicals produced commercially and to identify those that have the potential for causing cancer in people, based on their ability to cause mutations in genes. Chemicals identified in this way can then be tested more carefully in animals.

It is certainly reassuring to know that we do have ways of check-
ing out all of the thousands of new industrially produced chemicals
that constantly invade our lives. And we have been warned over and
over again that smoking and intense exposure to sunlight are serious cancer risks. But what adjustments should we make for the more
subtle lifestyle factors, such as diet and the use of alcohol? Let's talk
about diet and whether or not we really should pay attention to
those cereal commercials.

"We are what we eat" is an old and often quoted aphorism. Diet
and its relationship to cancer is a very complicated question and it is
not easy to definitively incriminate specific foods in the causation of
cancer. However, the results of a great many studies, including one
by the National Cancer Institute in the United States, which in 1980
established a special committee called the Committee on Diet, Nutrition, and Cancer, suggest that a diet which is likely to afford you op-
timal protection from cancer is one which is

low in fat,

low in calories,

low in salt,

high in fiber, and

high in fruits and green and yellow vegetables

One informative way of evaluating the influence of diet on cancer is to compare cancer incidence and cancer death rates in people
in different parts of the world who sustain different diets. Such comparisons indicate that people in Western countries, who derive as
much as half of their total dietary calories from fats, experience
a high mortality from cancer of the breast (in postmenopausal
women), colon, ovaries, prostate, pancreas, and womb, compared
to Japanese people, who typically derive much less of their calories

from fat. On the other hand, Japanese diets contain more salt than conventional Western diets, and this is reflected in a higher incidence of cancer of the stomach in the Japanese population.

The influence of diet on cancer has been extensively studied in experimental animals. Rodents that have unlimited access to food develop cancer more frequently, and also have shorter life spans in general, than animals with a diet that is restricted in calories. Interestingly, the benefits of a calorie-restricted diet in rodents are not confined to cancer that occurs spontaneously. These animals are also relatively more resistant to the carcinogenic effect of known cancer-causing chemicals added to their diet.

In the final analysis you certainly can't go wrong by maintaining a diet low in fat and calories and high in fresh fruits, grains and legumes, and vegetables—especially yellow vegetables—despite the fact that fruits and vegetables contain some chemical carcinogens.

In addition to the neutralization of cancer-causing chemicals, which we discussed in Question 15, we know that certain substances in the environment can actually protect our cells against the effects of such chemicals. Some of these substances are called *antimutagens* and *anticarcinogens,* and as I indicated in Question 10, certain natural foods and plants are known to contain quite large amounts of them. At the present time we don't know very much about how these substances work, and very few of them have actually been isolated and tested properly. But this is an extremely important and active area of cancer research.

Just as it is difficult to identify agents that cause particular cancers, so it is equally difficult to identify agents that protect against cancer. In the first place, different anticarcinogens and antimutagens are likely to be protective against only selected types of cancers, and it requires careful and very time-consuming analysis by cancer epidemiologists to corroborate this. For example, if a particular anticarcinogen present in a certain vegetable did in fact protect against stomach cancer but not against other types of cancer, it would be difficult to know this unless cancer epidemiologists were studying stomach cancer in a very careful way. And even if an astute epidemiologist did notice that in a particular population the incidence of cancer was dropping over a period of years, and confirmed this by statistical tests, it would still be very difficult to sort out the relationship of cancer of the stomach to eating a particular vegetable as opposed to some other variable in the lifestyle of that population of people, such as not drinking coffee, or even not snoring while sleeping. As it happens, the migration of storks over parts of Scandinavia actually does correlate with the peak months of childbirth. But that doesn't mean that storks bring babies!

In the same vein, it is often very difficult to prove by scientifically acceptable tests that suspected anticarcinogens really do work. For example, you might know about the suggestion that vitamin C is an anticarcinogen. This idea is certainly not without scientific foundation since vitamin C is known to be able to neutralize many of the waste products of normal cellular metabolism that I mentioned in Question 10, which are known to cause damage to the DNA of our cells. While the role of vitamin C in cancer prevention is still controversial, there is a wave of renewed interest in the scientific community in this and other chemicals that work in a similar way.

Why, then, don't we all routinely take large amounts af vitamin C or other suggested anticarcinogens and antimutagens every day? Before government agencies such as the U.S. Food and Drug Administration will sanction the use of any chemical for medical purposes, they appropriately require that there be good scientific evidence that the chemical really does do what it is supposed to do. This is a perfectly reasonable requirement, since otherwise you as a consumer would be wasting your money and, more important, possibly exposing yourself to other risks due to side effects. In the case of vitamin C in particular, which has few harmful effects, this may not be a significant problem (except for the intense indigestion that it might cause you). But in the case of other chemicals that are possible but not proven anticarcinogens, large doses might indeed be dangerous. You surely do not want to gobble lots of a potentially dangerous chemical unless you are pretty sure it's going to protect you against cancer. We'll return to this issue in Question 20 when we address the use of unproven and hence potentially dangerous substances for the treatment of cancer.

But even at this moment, efforts are under way by various approved agencies to rigorously test some of the more promising anticarcinogens. For example, there are suggestions that foods rich in vitamin A (which belongs to a family of chemical compounds called *retinoids*) protect against cancer. A study has been recently initiated among men who are at risk for lung cancer because they smoke, or work with high levels of asbestos, to determine whether vitamin A and a related substance called *beta carotene* (which gets its name from the fact that it is very abundant in carrots) really do help prevent cancer. (By the way, let me warn you that large amounts of beta carotene can be harmful, but you have to consume many pounds of carrots a day to suffer this risk.) The best sources of vitamin A are fish oils, dairy products (especially butter), liver, and eggs. Beta carotene is also abundant in yams, tomatoes, papayas, peaches, cantaloupe, spinach, and broccoli. In fact, it has been estimated that one serving of fresh broccoli (the amount present in one cup of the chopped vegetable) provides you with about 90 percent of your daily requirement of vitamin A. Additionally, this amount of broccoli will give you about twice the daily recommended amount of vitamin C, a lot of the minerals that your body needs, and about 25 percent of the daily amount of fiber your diet should have.

Thus far we have talked about chemicals called carcinogens— agents that cause cancer by messing up our DNA. But we also know that certain chemicals can increase the likelihood that a particular carcinogen will cause a cell to become cancerous, *even though by itself that chemical is not a carcinogen.* We call such agents *tumor promotors* because they can bring about the development of cancer by carcinogens. Essentially, they can turn a weak cancer-causing chemical into a much stronger one. We don't know exactly how tumor promotors work, but we do know that somehow in the presence of the damage caused by carcinogens, they increase the potential of cells to grow in a uncontrolled way. It is possible that some of the so-called lifestyle factors in cancer, such as diet and alcohol consumption, act as tumor promotors rather than as carcinogens. Unfortunately, in contrast to our ability to detect carcinogens in the environment by using the kinds of tests that I just mentioned, we don't yet have any tests for tumor promotors.

Drinking alcohol is a good example of how a tumor promotor might increase cancer risk. As you no doubt remember from school, the principal ingredient in booze is a chemical called ethanol. Now pure ethanol by itself does not cause damage to DNA, or mutations, or cancer. But the consumption of ethanol has been linked to different types of cancer in people. Its relationship to liver cancer is very clear, mainly because ethanol destroys the cells of the liver, making them much more prone to become cancerous by other factors. But in addition to liver cancer, a study on alcohol consumption and breast cancer showed that women who had between three and nine drinks a week had a 30 percent increased risk of breast cancer, and those who consumed more than nine drinks a week had a 60 percent increased risk of breast cancer.

Remember that these are the results of one single study, and that studies on factors such as diet and alcohol and coffee consumption are often contradictory because they are complicated by the issue of the presence of so many different variables and trying to sort out what's important and what's not. For instance, many people who drink alcohol like to smoke when they drink. The epidemiologists who carried out the study on breast cancer and its relationship to alcohol consumption excluded people who both smoke and drink. But researchers often are unable to know what other lifestyle factors may go along with drinking alcohol. Maybe you recall another recent study reported quite widely in the lay press which suggested that drinking coffee was a risk factor for cancer of the pancreas. This study suffered severe professional criticism, and it is by no means clear that drinking coffee has anything to do with pancreatic cancer.

So what's the bottom line? What should you believe and what shouldn't you believe? Here is some sane advice that you should follow as regularly as possible.

Don't smoke.

Avoid a lot of sun.

Don't drink excessively.

Avoid eating or drinking synthetic chemicals whenever possible.

Eat a balanced, healthy diet of the type discussed earlier.

Get plenty of exercise and stay as fit as possible.

These are certainly lifestyle practices that you can expect to decrease your chances of getting cancer. Above and beyond this *do everything in moderation and avoid all excesses*. We humans are the products of millions of years of evolution and during these eons of time our bodies have evolved very clever ways of dealing with many things in the world that can cause disease, including cancer, provided we are exposed to them infrequently and in small packages.

How do cancer treatments work?

18

Meet the disease at its first stage.
                                    —*Persius*

There are several ways of treating cancer. Let's start with surgical treatment. The concept here is quite simple. A surgeon removes the cancerous tissue by cutting it out with a knife. Surgical treatment can result in a complete cure if the surgeon is able to remove every single cancer cell. The greatest likelihood for this happy outcome is when the cancer is completely confined to a single tumor.

In many such cases, surgery is a very effective way of treating cancer, especially if the cancer is located in an accessible part of the body, so that the surgeon can reach all of the cancer and can safely remove a generous amount of the surrounding normal tissue, just to be certain. Cancer of the breast is often treated this way, frequently with very successful results. But it goes without saying that if the surgeon has to operate on a cancer growing in or near a vital organ like the brain or the heart, there are limits to how much of that organ can be removed without causing other kinds of problems. So sometimes a cancer may be *inoperable* because of where it is growing.

Another condition that can make a cancer inoperable is that it has spread to many parts of the body—in other words, the tumor has metastasized widely. Under such circumstances it is impossible to surgically remove all the cancerous tissue, especially if it is not clear just how widely the cancer has spread. Of course a third condition that can make cancer inoperable is that the patient's general health is not adequate to survive the ordeal of major surgery.

Unfortunately, it is not possible for a surgeon to know for sure that he has removed every single cancer cell, because very small numbers of cancer cells cannot be detected. In theory even a single cancer cell remaining in the body after surgery may be sufficient for the cancer to start growing again. For this reason it is very common to follow surgical treatment of cancer with some other type of treatment that is designed to kill any remaining cancer cells. Such nonsurgical treatments are also used in cases that cannot be effectively treated by surgery for the reasons mentioned above and in situations where other forms of treatment are considered to be more effective than surgery.

The two most widely used nonsurgical treatments involve the use of X-rays and chemicals to kill cancer cells. But wait a minute! Didn't we discuss the fact that X-rays and chemicals can cause damage to the DNA of cells and hence promote the development of cancer? This does indeed sound like a paradox, so let's try to resolve it before we go any further.

The problem that we face in deciding how to approach the nonsurgical treatment of cancer is to find a way of *selectively* killing cancer cells. The ideal cancer treatment would be one that kills cancer cells very effectively but *never* kills or harms normal cells. We'll talk a little more later about how such highly selective drugs might be designed in the future. But as yet we do not have such a perfect "magic bullet." So the next best thing is to try to kill cancer cells preferentially over normal cells, recognizing full well that in the process some normal cells will also be killed or at least seriously harmed.

One way of achieving this goal is to take advantage of the fact that cancer cells continually go through the process of cell division by which each cell gives rise to two new cells, which in turn each give rise to two more cells, and so on. This of course is the essence of the relentless exponential growth of cancer, as I explained earlier. If we can stop cells from dividing we can arrest the growth of the cancer. A very effective way of interfering with the ability of cancer cells to divide is to damage their DNA. Such damage not only causes changes in genes which alter their ability to make normal proteins, it also interferes with the process of making a new copy of the DNA when cells divide. If the DNA is not copied the cells cannot achieve the formation of new cells, because the DNA is the brain of the cell and cells cannot survive without it. Another way of interfering with DNA is to actually block the copying process. Think of a photocopying machine as an analogy. One way of making sure that the machine no longer copies documents is to damage some part of it. Another way is to cut off the supply of paper.

In order to damage DNA molecules and hence stop cancer cells from proliferating, we expose patients with cancer to agents that we know damage DNA, such as X-rays or chemicals, or sometimes both. The treatment of cancer with X-rays is called *radiation therapy* (or *radiotherapy*) and the treatment of cancer with chemicals is called *chemotherapy*. So what about the paradox? Well, there really isn't one. Agents that damage DNA are very effective for killing cells, especially when used in the high amounts that are employed in cancer treatment. And while it is true that these same agents can indeed cause cancer in normal cells, the risk from radiation therapy or chemotherapy is in fact only slightly increased. If you have cancer right now and your immediate survival is at stake, your benefits from cancer treatment far outweigh the slightly increased risk of another type of cancer ten or twenty years from now. In fact, we have been using radiation therapy and chemotherapy long enough now to know that this risk is very small.

A far more serious problem than the possibility of getting a different cancer because of radiation therapy or chemotherapy is the immediate effect of these agents on normal cells of the body that are also dividing and hence have to duplicate their DNA frequently.

Remember that cells are continually being replaced as they are lost from the surface of the skin and from the intestine and lungs and uterus and other places. And cells in the bone marrow are constantly dividing in order to make new red and white blood cells. Even though only a small fraction of the approximately three trillion cells in the body actively grow (divide), these cells are very important for your health, and serious complications can result if they are killed in large numbers by cancer treatments.

The effect of cancer treatment on the bone marrow is particularly important. As I indicated earlier, the marrow of our bones is a place where all our red and white blood cells are made, and millions of these cells pour out of our marrow into our bloodstream every day. The red blood cells deliver oxygen, which they pick up from the air in our lungs, to every part of the body. The white cells are part of the immune system that we discussed earlier, which protects us from being overwhelmed by invading foreign cells like bacteria and other nasties. The bone marrow also makes a third type of cell called *platelets*, which are required for blood to clot properly whenever we bleed.

Red cells, most white cells, and platelets have a very short life span in the bloodstream and as they die they must be continually replaced. When a person is treated for cancer with radiation therapy or chemotherapy, these dividing bone marrow cells get into the same difficulty that cancer cells do, and many of them die. As a result fewer new red cells are made and that is why treatment for cancer often makes people feel very weak and tired. Similarly, the depletion of white cells compromises the immune system, and patients on chemotherapy or radiation therapy are much more prone to all sorts of infections. And of course the loss of platelets increases the risk of bleeding problems.

Although injury to the bone marrow is one of the more serious complications of cancer treatment it is not the only one. Any cells that are usually dividing are at risk. For example, the normal process of replacing cells in the intestines is interfered with and that's why intestinal problems like nausea, vomiting, and diarrhea are common complications of chemotherapy. Another common complication is that the growth of cells in the hair follicles is affected, resulting in a loss of hair.

A great many chemicals are available for use in chemotherapy and I won't attempt to list them all here. But you might want to know the names of some of the chemicals used most frequently, in case you encounter them in your reading or discussions with doctors.

CHEMICALS USED IN CANCER CHEMOTHERAPY

Those That Damage DNA	*Those That Interfere With Making New DNA*
Alkylating agents	Arabinosylcytosine (AraC)
Nitrosoureas	Hydroxyurea
Cis platin	6-Thioguanine
Bleomycin	6-Mercaptopurine
Adriamycin	5-Fluorouracil
Daunorubicin	Methotrexate
Dactinomycin	
Plicamycin	
Mitomycin	

It is important to realize that nowadays the use of radiotherapy and chemotherapy is very sophisticated and is designed to minimize the risk of complications. For example, in many cases the use of elaborate machines and very clever computers makes it possible to target the delivery of X-rays to exactly and exclusively that part of the body where cancer cells are present or might remain after surgery, therefore avoiding damage to normal cells, especially bone marrow cells. In addition, medicines are available to help deal with the complications of depletion of bone marrow cells and with other complications if they arise. So once again, on balance, the benefits of radiation therapy and chemotherapy far outweigh the risks.

In recent years an innovative approach to the problem of bone marrow damage during radiation therapy or chemotherapy has led to a new form of cancer treatment called *bone marrow transplantation*. In this treatment a person with cancer is given very high doses of chemicals—enough to kill many more cancer cells than is possible with conventional radiation therapy. These high doses cause so much damage to the bone marrow that without some other treatment the marrow simply could not recover and the patient would be left with absolutely no blood cells. This problem is overcome by giving the patient a transfusion (*transplant*) of perfectly normal bone marrow. Ideally, the patient is given his or her own bone marrow cells back (*autologous bone marrow transplant*) by removing and storing marrow cells before the treatment. But sometimes this isn't possible because the patient's marrow may already be seriously depleted of cells from radiation therapy or chemotherapy, or he may have cancer cells growing in his marrow, in which case there is obviously little point in removing and storing it. In these situations bone marrow cells are taken from someone else, a healthy donor (*heterologous bone marrow transplant*). Cells from the donor's marrow are able to seed in the patient and replenish his bone marrow very effectively.

But one cannot get bone marrow cells from just anyone. You will remember from an earlier discussion that whenever cells from one person are introduced into another person's body they are recognized as being foreign and are killed by the immune system. That's why bone marrow transplantation works best if the patient can be given back his or her own stored marrow. However, the extent to which the immune system recognizes cells as foreign depends on how related or unrelated that person is. The cells of identical twins are in fact exactly the same and are not rejected at all, and cells from a brother or sister are not as foreign as cells from an unrelated individual. So in circumstances where the patient cannot be given back his own marrow, bone marrow transplantation uses marrow from a donor who is closely "matched" to the recipient. Of course the ideal donor is an identical twin, but usually siblings, and even other close relatives, have cells that are sufficiently like the cells of the patient for the new bone marrow cells to be frequently accepted and tolerated. When a close relative is nonexistent or not readily available, the general population is searched to find a person who by chance has bone marrow cells that match—that is, are similar to—those of the patient in need. In order to match bone marrow cells certain biochemical characteristics of the cells that are genetically determined are compared, much the same way that blood types are compared for conventional blood transfusions.

Bone marrow transplantation is especially well suited for cancer which affects cells in the marrow itself, such as leukemia. Massive destruction of the bone marrow by chemical treatment can effectively kill all the cancer cells and the person can then receive "new" marrow and be totally cured. Leukemia is a good example of a situation in which the patient cannot be given his or her own stored marrow because it is cancerous.

Like all forms of treatment for cancer, bone marrow transplantation is not without problems and complications. Among the most serious is the fact that sometimes the transplanted marrow cells from a different person begin to recognize the patient's own cells as being foreign, and a form of rejection happens in which the donated cells essentially begin to kill the patient! Additionally, after exposure to the very large doses of agents used to kill the cancer cells there is a short time period before the transplanted bone marrow cells have had sufficient time to take over the production of sufficient numbers of red and white blood cells and platelets. During this time the patient is essentially devoid of any normal bone marrow function.

His own marrow has been completely knocked out, and the transplanted marrow is not yet working at full strength. Not unexpectedly, patients are very vulnerable to various complications during this time, particularly infections which cannot be dealt with because of the lack of an adequate immune system.

You should be aware that treatments like bone marrow transplantation are still very much in the development stage and are highly specialized. Not every hospital has the ability to perform such treatment and some places are more recognized for their expertise and experience than others. Be sure to seek out competent advice about where such treatment is best available. Recognize too that compared to other more conventional types of treatment, the treatment of cancer by bone marrow transplantation is very expensive and may require a considerable personal financial commitment. Some insurance carriers may consider bone marrow transplantation experimental and may not reimburse health care facilities the considerable cost of this treatment.

In addition to surgery, chemotherapy, and radiation therapy, some particular types of cancer can be treated in very specialized ways. These forms of treatment take advantage of the fact that the growth of some cancer cells depends on the presence of special factors in the body. Once again, breast cancer provides a good example. The normal growth of cells in the breast is influenced by certain hormones, particularly the hormone *estrogen,* which is manufactured in the ovary and which stimulates breast cells to divide. In *some* (but not all) types of breast cancer the cancer cells are quite dependent on the presence of estrogen in order to grow. So if the supply of estrogen to these cells can somehow be cut off the cancer cells won't grow as quickly. Recently a chemical called *tamoxifen* has been shown to interfere with the ability of breast cancer cells to take up estrogen. In fact, this compound looks so promising in the *prevention* of breast cancer that at the time of this writing a massive study of its usefulness, involving 16,000 women, is being planned.

CANCER ANSWERS

The general idea of interfering with the growth of cancer cells by using hormones which these cells need in order to grow can sometimes also be applied to the treatment of certain types of cancer of the prostate gland. In this case estrogen actually interferes with the growth of the cancer cells, and so this hormone is sometimes administered to men with prostatic cancer.

Who can help me make decisions about cancer treatment?

19

The healthy, the strong individual,
is the one who asks for help
when he needs it.

—*Rona Barrett*

When one has been diagnosed with cancer one is sometimes forced to make decisions about treatment that are difficult under any circumstances, and are particularly difficult at a time when one is struggling to deal with a severe emotional shock. Patients are understandably bewildered by a whole host of choices and decisions. Which of several possible recommended treatments should I have? When must I start treatment? Should I get a second or even a third opinion? Where should I have my treatment carried out?

Every person with cancer is a unique individual and is given individual and sometimes unique advice. So no doctor who has never examined you, and certainly no book, can give you informed opinions about your particular case. I certainly don't presume to here. But in attempting to answer the question about decisions for cancer treatment I will try to give you useful general advice and reassurance, and I'll use some examples of the results of cancer treatment.

The issue of where to have treatment such as surgery, radiotherapy, or chemotherapy is sometimes of considerable concern to patients with cancer. Is my local hospital adequate? Should I travel to a "famous" medical center, possibly even out of the country? I don't have simple definitive answers to these questions; nobody does. But I would suggest that you seek out mature and experienced advice and use your own common sense. Quite obviously, the larger and more comprehensive the medical facility, the greater the likelihood of its ability to deliver state-of-the-art treatment. It is true that certain medical centers and hospitals have special experience in the treatment of certain types of cancer. If this is generally recognized in your medical community you can expect to receive such recommendations from most doctors and oncologists. But in general the great majority of major medical facilities, certainly those in all major cities and even fairly large towns, are extremely well equipped to handle the treatment of most types of cancer. *Surgery, radiation therapy and chemotherapy are now pretty standard treatments in most parts of the world.*

You might hear about facilities in various parts of the country that are called comprehensive cancer centers. Many of these are affiliated with prominent medical schools. The term "comprehensive" is not meant to imply that these centers are unique in the breadth or completeness of the treatment they offer. Rather, the term refers to the fact that they specialize in the diagnosis and treatment of cancer and also that they have extensive cancer research programs. There are also facilities that are not designated as comprehensive centers because they are devoted exclusively either to research or clinical treatment. The following is a list of some of these comprehensive and noncomprehensive centers, organized alphabetically for your easy reference.

CANCER CENTERS

Albert Einstein College of
  Medicine Cancer Research
  Center
Chanin Building, Room 330
1300 Morris Park Avenue
Bronx, New York 10461
(212) 430-2302

American Health Foundation
320 East 43rd Street
New York, NY 10017
(212) 953-1900 (ex 212)

Armand Hammer Center
  for Cancer Biology
Salk Institute
P.O. Box 85800
San Diego, CA 92186-5800
(619) 453-4100 (ex 386)

Bowman Gray School of Medicine
Wake Forest University
300 South Hawthorne Road
Winston-Salem, NC 27103
(919) 748-4464

Brown University
825 Chalkstone Avenue
Providence, RI 02908
(401) 456-2661

California Institute of
Technology Cancer Center
Biology Division 147-75
Pasadena, CA 91125
(818) 397-2762

Case Western Reserve University
Ireland Cancer Center
2074 Abington Road
Cleveland, OH 44106
(216) 844-8453

City of Hope National
Medical Center
Beckman Research Institute
1450 East Duarte Road
Duarte, CA 91010
(818) 359-8111 (ex 2704)

Cold Spring Harbor Laboratory
P.O. Box 100
Cold Spring Harbor, NY 11724
(516) 367-8310

Columbia University College of
Physicians and Surgeons
Cancer Center
701 West 168th Street, Room 1601
New York, NY 10032
(212) 305-6730

Dana-Farber Cancer Institute
44 Binney Street
Boston, MA 02115
(617) 732-3636

Detroit Comprehensive
Cancer Center
110 East Warren Street
Detroit, MI 48201
(313) 833-0710

Drew-Meharry-Morehouse
Consortium Cancer Center
1005 D.B. Todd Boulevard
Nashville, TN 37208
(615) 327-6315

Duke University Medical Center
Duke Comprehensive
Cancer Center
Jones Research Building,
Box 3843
Research Drive, Room 228
Durham, NC 27710
(919) 684-3377

Emory University School
of Medicine
Goodwin Institute for
Cancer Research
Atlanta, GA 30322
(404) 727-4283

Fels Research Institute
Temple University School
of Medicine
3420 North Broad Street
Philadelphia, PA 19140
(215) 221-4019

Fox Chase Cancer Center
7701 Burholme Avenue
Philadelphia, PA 19111
(215) 728-2781

Fred Hutchinson Cancer
  Research Center
1124 Columbia Street
Seattle, WA 98104
(206) 467-4675

Frederick Cancer
  Research Center
National Cancer Institute
P.O. Box B
Frederick, MD 21702
(301) 846-1000

Georgetown University
  Medical Center
Lombardi Cancer
  Research Center
3800 Reservoir Road, N.W.
Washington, D.C. 20007
(202) 625-2042

Illinois Cancer Council
200 South Michigan Avenue
Room 1700
Chicago, IL 60604-2404
(312) 226-2379

Johns Hopkins Oncology Center
600 North Wolfe Street,
  Room 157
Baltimore, MD 21205
(301) 955-8638

Jonsson Comprehensive
  Cancer Center
University of California
  at Los Angeles, Factor Building
10833 LeConte Avenue
Los Angeles, CA 90024-1781
(213) 825-5268

Kenneth Norris, Jr.
  Comprehensive Cancer Center
University of Southern California
P.O. Box 33800
Los Angeles, CA 90033-0800
(213) 224-6465

La Jolla Cancer Research
  Foundation
10901 North Torrey Pines Road
La Jolla, CA 92037
(619) 455-6480

Massachusetts Institute
  of Technology Center for
  Cancer Research
Room E17-529B
Cambridge MA 02139
(617) 253-6400

Mayo Clinic
Mayo Comprehensive
  Cancer Center
200 First Street, S.W.
Rochester, MN 55905
(507) 284-3413

McArdle Laboratory for
  Cancer Research
University of Wisconsin
1400 University Avenue,
  Room 1009
Madison, WI 53706
(608) 262-2177

Mount Sinai Cancer Center
One Gustave L. Levy Place
New York, NY 10029
(212) 241-6500

New England Deaconess Hospital
Cancer Research Institute
Shields Warren
  Radiation Laboratory
185 Pilgrim Road
Boston, MA 02215
(617) 732-8536

New York University
  Medical Center
Cancer Center
550 First Avenue
New York, NY 10016
(212) 263-5927

Norris Cotton Cancer Center
Dartmouth-Hitchcock
  Medical Center
2 Maynard Street, HB7920
Hanover, NH 03756
(603) 646-5505

Ohio State University
Comprehensive Cancer Center
410 W. 12th Avenue, Suite 302
Columbus, OH 43210
(614) 293-8619

Pittsburgh Cancer Institute
University of Pittsburgh
200 Meyran Avenue
Pittsburgh, PA 15213-2592
(412) 647-2072

Purdue University
Hansen Life Sciences
  Research Building
West Lafayette, IN 47907
(317) 494-9129

Roswell Park Memorial Institute
666 Elm Street
Buffalo, NY 14263
(716) 845-4400

Sloan-Kettering Cancer Center
1275 York Avenue
New York, NY 10021
(212) 794-5845

St. Jude Children's
  Research Hospital
332 North Lauderdale
Memphis, TN 38105
(901) 522-0301

The Jackson Laboratory
600 Main Street
Bar Harbor, ME 04609-0800
(207) 288-3371 (ex 1206)

The Wistar Institute
  Cancer Center
36th Street at Spruce
Philadelphia, PA 19104-4268
(215) 898-3703 or 3926

University of Alabama/
  Birmingham
Comprehensive Cancer Center
University Station
1824 Sixth Avenue South,
  Room 214
Birmingham, AL 35294
(205) 934-6612

University of Arizona College
  of Medicine Cancer Center
1501 North Campbell Avenue
Tucson, AZ 85724
(602) 626-7925

University of California
  at San Diego Medical Center
Cancer Center, T010
225 Dickinson Street
San Diego, CA 92103
(619) 534-1501

University of Chicago
  Cancer Research Center
5841 South Maryland Avenue
Box 444
Chicago, IL 60637
(312) 702-6180

University of Colorado
  Health Sciences Center
Cancer Center
4200 East 9th Avenue, Box B171
Denver, CO 80262
(303) 270-8801

University of Michigan
  Cancer Center
101 Simpson Drive
Ann Arbor, MI 48109-0752
(313) 936-2516

University of Miami Medical School
Sylvester Comprehensive
  Cancer Center
1475 N.W.12th Avenue
Miami, FL 33101
(305) 548-4810

University of Nebraska
  Medical Center
Eppley Institute for
  Cancer Research
600 South 42nd Street
Omaha, NE 68198-6805
(402) 559-4238

University of North Carolina
  School of Medicine
Cancer Research Center
  CB-7295
Chapel Hill, NC 27599-7295
(919) 966-3036

University of Pennsylvania
  Cancer Center
6th Floor Penn Tower
3400 Spruce Street
Philadelphia, PA 19104-4283
(215) 662-6334

University of Rochester
  Cancer Center
601 Elmwood Avenue
Box 704
Rochester, NY 14642
(716) 275-4911

University of Texas
  M.D. Anderson Cancer Center
1515 Holcombe Boulevard
Houston, TX 77030
(713) 792-6000

University of Virginia Medical
  Center Cancer Center
Box 334
Charlottesville, VA 22908
(804) 924-5111

University of Wisconsin Clinical
  Cancer Center
600 Highland Avenue
Madison, WI 53792
(608) 263-8600

Utah Regional Cancer Center
University of Utah Medical Center
50 North Medical Drive
Salt Lake City, UT 84132
(801) 581-8793

Wayne State University
Meyer L. Prentis Comprehensive
  Cancer of Metropolitan Detroit
3990 John R. Street, 1 Brush S.
Detroit, MI 48201
(313) 745-8870

Vermont Regional Cancer Center
University of Vermont
1 South Prospect Street
Burlington, VT 05401-3498
(802) 656-4414

Worcester Foundation
  for Experimental Biology
222 Maple Avenue
Shrewsbury, MA 01545
(508) 842-8921

Virginia Commonwealth
  University
Medical College of Virginia
MCV Station, Box 230
Richmond, VA 23298
(804) 786-9722

Yale University School of
  Medicine Comprehensive
  Cancer Center
333 Cedar Street,
  Room WWW 205
New Haven, CT 06510
(203) 785-6338

Doctors who perform cancer surgery and who administer radio-therapy and chemotherapy have specialized training. In fact the treatment of cancer by using radiation is a particular discipline of medicine called *radiation oncology*. These specialists are highly trained in special surgical procedures and in the use of radiation and chemicals for the treatment of cancer. In addition, they are often actively engaged in research on safer and more effective ways of delivering cancer treatment, and the development of safer and more effective new treatments. A little later we will talk about some new and innovative ways of treating cancer that hold promise for the future.

It is also important to understand that if one is treated with radiotherapy or chemotherapy instead of surgery, it does not nec-essarily mean that one's cancer is inoperable and therefore more advanced. After many years of trials with different ways of treating cancer, oncologists have learned that certain types of cancers are better suited to certain types of treatments than others. Some types of cancer cells are extremely sensitive to X-rays and the cancer responds very dramatically to radiation therapy. Other tumors do not respond well to this form of treatment. The same is true for chemotherapy. Here the options are even greater because oncologists have a large arsenal of different chemicals available to them. I gave you an abbreviated list of just some of these chemicals earlier. Some work better on some tumors than others and sometimes particular combinations of chemicals or of a chemical plus radiation, work best of all.

In the final analysis it is frequently the case that multiple options are available for the treatment of a particular cancer because experience has shown that they are equally likely to produce similar results. So don't be surprised if different doctors give you different opinions and recommendations for treatment. This doesn't necessarily mean that one or more of them is wrong. The treatment of almost all types of cancer is in a constant state of evaluation in order to try to improve it. But these evaluations are almost never comparisons between treatments that work and treatments that don't work. They are between treatments that work as well as we know how, and treatments that may possibly work a little better. If you are given different opinions for treatment it does not mean that one of them will cure your cancer and the others won't. If there is a single definitive treatment that is much better than any other, you can be sure you will be told about it. When doctors provide recommendations for treatment they consider each individual case and take many different factors into account that are relevant to each individual patient. These factors include an assessment of what type of cancer is present, where it is present, how localized it is, how old the patient is, his or her general state of health, and many other factors. Based on this comprehensive evaluation some oncologists may recommend a particular surgical treatment; others may prefer a different surgical treatment, or may suggest radiotherapy or chemotherapy, and yet others may suggest combinations of these.

A good illustrative example of different treatments that produce the same results is the treatment of breast cancer. Based on the results of the treatment of women with the same type of breast cancer at the same *early* stage of development, a number of studies have shown that the chances of being cured were the same in women who had an entire breast removed, a procedure called *total mastectomy*, or had just the part of the breast removed that included the entire cancer lump, a procedure called a *lumpectomy*. So in cases of early breast cancer, the predominant recommended treatment nowadays is usually conservative surgery (lumpectomy) plus radiotherapy. However, in some studies the results of the lumpectomy were the same whether or not the patients also had radiotherapy after the surgical treatment. But remember this is not the whole story in the treatment of breast cancer. The situation changes depending on whether or not the cancer has spread to lymph nodes and can also change depending on the age of the person. Each case is individual! In situations in which breast cancer has spread to the neighboring lymph nodes, or to the surrounding tissues such as the underlying muscle, it is usually necessary to carry out more extensive surgery. Such a procedure is called *radical mastectomy*. Radical mastectomy used to be the preferred method for the treatment of most, if not all, breast cancer. However, the observation that less disfiguring surgery works just as well in many cases, has led to a decline in the use of this form of surgical treatment in many parts of the world.

Doctors know and understand that the diagnosis of cancer is a terrible psychological burden for patients and their families. And you as a patient or a family member have every right to expect this understanding. So it is perfectly reasonable to consult more than one medical opinion about a particular cancer treatment. But remember, provided that the opinions come from reputable physicians who have experience in the treatment of cancer, the issue is not one of deciding between the right and wrong treatments. The issue is the availability of different treatments. Try to appreciate that while your doctor can and should give you every possible advice, he or she cannot make final decisions for you. You have to make treatment decisions for yourself based on the recommendations you receive. Recognize too that the pressure for making decisions quickly and for getting on with treatment is motivated by the need to begin the process of killing cancer cells as soon as possible. Once the disease is diagnosed it surely does not make sense to waste time before starting treatment. *This does not mean that one cannot delay things for a few days to seek other advice.* But most certainly one should not delay treatment of cancer any longer than is necessary.

What are
alternative
cancer
treatments?

20

*I observe the physician with the same diligence
as he the disease.*

—*John Donne*

When people are afflicted with diseases that might be fatal, such as cancer, it is completely understandable that they will be strongly tempted to turn to any and all sources of possible help, no matter how unaccepted or unconventional they are in the medical world. I want to offer a few words of caution and advice about questionable and so-called *alternative cancer treatments*. The paranoid idea is sometimes bandied about that compound X or Y does indeed cure cancer, but is not used as a conventional treatment because it works so well that it will put "them" (all doctors) out of business. It's only available in some remote corner of the world and you'd better get on a plane to get it as soon as possible. It is really quite absurd even to contemplate the idea that the medical profession, the pharmaceutical industry, or any other organized group related to health care has a vested interest against finding a cure for cancer. As has been pointed out in an illuminating article on this topic written by the president of an organization called the National Council Against Health Fraud, many victims of cancer and their families are health professionals themselves and have as much interest in curing cancer as anyone else.

Additionally, there is no precedent for any sort of financial imperatives to suppress the development of any type of promising treatment for any disease anywhere in the world. A pertinent example quoted in the article mentioned above is that the elimination of polio by the discovery of a vaccine rendered the entire iron lung industry obsolete virtually overnight, without so much as a whimper. (The iron lung was an elaborate and expensive artificial breathing machine that kept polio victims alive.) Believe me, the manufacturers of sophisticated and expensive machines for delivering radiation therapy would accept the same inevitable consequence if a pill that cured cancer was discovered tomorrow.

Rumors of questionable and scientifically unsubstantiated treatments for all sorts of diseases circulate frequently. And those who are suffering from diseases that may sometimes be incurable, such as cancer, understandably cling to the hope that such treatments may indeed work for them. And, of course, this is most likely to be the case when conventional treatments do not appear to be working. At the outset let's make the important distinction between alternative cancer treatments that are unsubstantiated by scientific testing, and those that have genuine scientific merit but which are experimental and still in the testing and evaluation stage. With respect to the latter category, as I mentioned earlier new approaches to the treatment of cancer are constantly under development and we'll discuss some specific examples when we address the question of the future of cancer treatment in Question 23. Many oncologists, particularly those working in medical centers with cancer research programs, are aware of these developments and may even be actively working on them themselves. Under certain circumstances, depending on the particular cancer in question, and on many other factors that the oncologist will know about, they may even be able to arrange for the participation of cancer patients in such studies. But when this happens it is always with the clear understanding that the treatment is experimental in nature, and all risks and conditions for participating in such experiments are carefully explained in advance.

The questionable alternative "cures" for cancer are not endorsed by health professionals but are touted by various lay groups, and sometimes regrettably, by true charlatans. The reputation of such "cures" depends on anecdotal claims for their success. A classic example of such a cancer treatment which fortunately is far less prevalent today than fifteen or twenty years ago is a substance called laetrile.

Laetrile (also known as amygdalin) is a cyanide-containing drug made from apricot kernels or the seeds of other related fruits. During the 1950s laetrile was touted as an agent effective in both the treatment and prevention of cancer. However, extensive testing and retesting by several government agencies failed to provide any evidence of its therapeutic efficacy. On the contrary, several studies concluded that it could be quite harmful for a variety of reasons, not the least being its potential for releasing cyanide in the body when taken by mouth. So the use of laetrile in the United States has never been approved by the Food and Drug Administration. Laetrile gained considerable national and international attention when lawsuits were filed to sanction the legal use of the compound for cancer treatment and by 1978 it was estimated that as many as 75,000 Americans had acquired it through the "cancer underground" and used it in attempts to either cure or prevent cancer.

But surely, you might ask, there is nothing to be lost by trying these unproven remedies? Nothing could be further from the truth. In the first place any treatment that has not been carefully and competently evaluated has the potential for side effects that may actually do one harm, as was convincingly shown for laetrile. Second, even if the "treatments" are not in themselves harmful, a serious consequence of their use, and one that is insufficiently recognized by cancer patients and their families, is that *those who use them are wasting valuable time*—time for continuing accepted forms of cancer treatment (which are frequently abandoned in favor of more questionable approaches), time for adjusting to the reality of their mortality, and time for progressing through the painful but necessary psychological stages which begin with shock and denial, but which in time mature to the acceptance of having a fatal disease. We must all eventually leave this existence called life and in our rational and collected moments, we all hope to do so in peace and with as much dignity as we can possibly muster. Peace and dignity are only achieved through the real acceptance of our mortality.

What are my chances of surviving cancer?

21

*One does not know—cannot know—
the best that is in one.*

—*Friedrich Nietzsche*

With increasing experience in the use of radiation and chemicals and with the ever larger repertoire of drugs available to the medical community for treating cancer, results are improving very steadily. There are some types of cancers that can be completely cured in a high percentage of cases. This includes cancers of the testicles and certain leukemias and lymphomas. And the treatment of some forms of breast and lung cancer, which both had a very bad outlook for many years, is now yielding very encouraging results.

We have to be careful about how we use the word "cure" in relation to cancer. As I indicated earlier, there is no way of knowing that any treatment has completely eliminated every cancer cell in the body. In theory even one single remaining cell can give rise to recurrence of the cancer. So it is not unusual for people to be apparently well for varying periods after treatment—a time called *remission*— only to relapse with the disease. However, after many years of treating people suffering from different types of cancer and observing how long they survived, it is possible to predict with a high degree of certainty that if one survives longer than the generally expected time for that type of cancer in the absence of further treatment, one can be considered to be cured, meaning that it is unlikely that the cancer will ever return. Obviously the longer one survives, the greater is the likelihood that the cancer is indeed truly cured, and, as I just indicated, the really good news is that this is happening more and more frequently.

The following table shows the steady improvement in the five year *relative survival rate* for some of the commoner types of cancers that were diagnosed in the United States during five periods from 1960 and 1985. These five-year survival rates have been mathemati-

Trends in Five-Year Survival Rates of Cancer

Site	1960–63	1970–73	1974–76	1977–79	1980–85	5–10 Year Relative Rate
All types	39%	43%	50%	50%	51%	84%
Testes	63	72	78	88	91	98
Uterus	73	81	89	87	83	98
Melanoma	60	68	79	81	81	89
Bladder	53	61	73	75	78	86
Breast	63	68	75	75	76	82
Prostate	50	63	67	71	73	71
Cervix	58	64	69	68	67	90
Colon	43	49	50	52	55	89
Rectum	38	45	48	50	53	84
Leukemia	14	22	34	36	34	61
Lung	8	10	12	13	13	70

Cancers are ranked according to survival rates for the period 1980–85.

The figures provided are for whites. Survival figures for Afro-Americans in the United States are not as complete for the earlier years and hence trends are less obvious. However, in general survival rates for Afro-Americans are approximately 5–10 percent lower.

The five- to ten-year relative survival rates are for cancers diagnosed during the period 1973–75 and are for all races.

cally adjusted *relative to the general population* so that they don't include deaths that would have been expected from other causes. They reflect the chance of escaping death strictly due to cancer for a five-year period. To state this more simply, to evaluate the effectiveness of a cancer treatment by asking how long a group of people live after the treatment, we want to be sure that we don't get confused by deaths that occurred from other diseases that people of that age might be expected to die of, such as heart disease. To avoid this complication we find out how many people of this age are expected to die of heart disease, and we adjust the survival figures to exclude these deaths. The last column of the table indicates what the chances are of surviving up to ten years after the diagnosis of cancer if one has already survived five years. Once again the survival rates were calculated as *relative* rates—the chance of escaping death solely due to cancer.

For example, the table shows that a person who was diagnosed with testicular cancer between 1960 and 1963 had a 63 percent chance of surviving five years after the treatment that was used at that time. But if a man was diagnosed with testicular cancer between the years 1980 and 1985 he had a 91 percent chance of surviving for five years after treatment. Quite clearly the treatment (and possibly also the early diagnosis) of testicular cancer improved considerably over that twenty-year period.

The table also shows that in general the chance of surviving for five years after the diagnosis of many other types of cancer is gradually improving. In some cases, such as cancer of the testes (testicles) and breast the chances of being cured are excellent. Unfortunately with cancer of the lung the prognosis is not as good. This doesn't mean that lung cancer cells don't respond to treatment. It more likely reflects the fact that it is still very difficult to diagnose lung cancer at an early stage when treatment can be effective. It is also evident from the table that if one survives any type of cancer for five years, the chances of surviving for another five years are very good, even in

Five-Year Survival of American Children Diagnosed with Cancer Before the Age of 15

Year	Survival (%)
1973	50.4
1974	53.4
1975	55.0
1976	56.6
1977	59.5
1978	63.7
1979	62.0
1980	62.5
1981	63.4

The year 1981 is the latest information available because we are always working with numbers that only emerge five years later. However, based on this steady improvement in five-year survival over a nine-year period, we can predict with a high degree of certainty that childhood cancers that were diagnosed in 1990 will have a five-year survival rate of about 79 percent.

the case of lung cancer. That is why five years of survival is generally used to indicate cure.

Similarly encouraging results have emerged for childhood cancer diagnosed before the age of 15. The following table shows the five-year survival for all childhood cancers in the United States from 1973 to 1981.

It is extremely important to understand that these survival rates reflect *probabilities* for survival time based on *large groups of individuals lumped together for statistical purposes*. So these numbers should not be individualized. Let's return to the relatively disappointing results for the treatment of lung cancer. These results are the average of many hundreds or even thousands of cases. But the results for any single person will depend (among other things) on just how advanced lung cancer is in that particular person.

Imagine that we have a sack with 10,000 beads that are absolutely identical except for the fact that 8,700 of them are white and 1,300 of them are red. If we reach in and grab handfuls of exactly 100 beads, most of the time 87 of them (or a number close to 87) will be white, and most of the time 13 (or a number close to 13) will be red. That's what we mean by *statistical probability*. But this situation holds only if there are no other differences between the red and white beads that might influence their selection in each handful. Imagine that the red beads are much smaller than the white beads. Now when we pick out handfuls of exactly 100 beads we are likely to find that more than 13 are red, because they occupy less space in one's hand than the white beads.

Likewise, if we consider 10,000 cases of lung cancer as if they were all the same and randomly sort them into 100 groups of 100 (for example, by giving each case a number and simply selecting numbers), we will find that the five-year survival rate for every group of 100 cases is approximately the same; about 13 percent. But if we pay attention to the fact that these cases are in fact different, and if we sort the 10,000 cases into 100 groups based on these differences, some groups of 100 cases will include many more than 13 people who survived for five years and some will include fewer than 13 people who survived this long. In reality this is indeed the case. Some cases of lung cancer are diagnosed early and are very confined when diagnosed. The prognosis for these particular cases is much better than for cases where lung cancer is diagnosed late or is more extensive. Furthermore, different types of lung cancer respond differently to different types of treatment. As a matter of fact, between 1985 and 1988 the three-year survival rate for cases of lung cancer that were localized and treated by surgery was close to 70 percent.

The same holds true for breast cancer in women and for colon cancer in both men and women. Earlier in the book we discussed how breast cancer is staged according to the size of the cancer and the extent of its spread. Stage 1 cancer of the breast has a five-year survival rate of about 80 percent. But this survival drops to 65 percent with stage 2 breast cancer, to 40 percent for stage 3 and to 10 percent with stage 4. Similarly, cancer of the colon that is strictly localized, as in stages A and B, has a 75 percent three-year survival rate. This drops to about 56 percent for stage C and to 15 percent with stage D.

It is difficult to make meaningful evaluations of cure rates for many different types of cancer if we introduce too many variables in the comparison, and so most often we combine all cases of a particular cancer to make these comparisons. So keep in mind that the purpose of presenting these numbers to you is largely to convince you that cancer cures *in general* are steadily improving.

Why don't treatments for cancer always result in a cure?

22

*Success and failure run contrary to expectation
sometimes in every disease.*
—Peter Mere Latham

Why is it that certain cancers can be cured and not others? In addition to the treatment of cancer, it is important to remember that the time of diagnosis has an important impact on cure. The earlier that any type of cancer is diagnosed, the greater the likelihood that it has not yet spread, hence the greater the likelihood that treatment will be effective. And of course there are many factors that contribute to the time of diagnosis. We discussed earlier the fact that cancer that develops as a lump in the breast or in the skin may be discovered early because these are very accessible parts of the body, whereas cancer of the stomach or lung may be quite extensive before it is discovered. In the same vein, if one ignores symptoms or delays seeking medical advice for ill health there is the risk that one might be delaying the diagnosis and treatment of cancer.

But with respect to cancer treatment itself, a major problem that affects the chances of a cure is that cancer cells can become resistant to agents that are designed to kill them. Let's talk a little more about this important problem of resistance to treatment and how it develops. When we talk about normal cells, part of what we mean is that cells in the body are very predictable and very uniform in their behavior. For example, every time a cell in the stomach divides, the daughter cells that emerge from this division look (under the microscope) and function like typical stomach cells. They don't suddenly change into brain cells or bone marrow cells or skin cells. This is true of all normal cells. They breed true. The reason for this is that each new cell inherits from its parent the correct pattern of precisely which genes should be switched to ON and OFF in that particular kind of cell and hence which protein machines should be working in that cell.

One of the most bothersome features of cancer cells is that they frequently change. A population of cancer cells is not uniform. New cancer cells do not always look or behave exactly as their parents do. In contrast to normal cells, cancer cells forget how to switch particular genes ON and OFF at the right time. Cancer cells are unstable. One of the consequences of this instability is that cancer cells are able to change in ways that allow them to outwit our efforts to kill them.

How do they do this? Let's look more closely at how chemotherapy works. When a chemical designed to kill cancer cells by damaging its DNA is injected or swallowed, it eventually passes into the bloodstream, as do all chemicals that are taken into the body. In order for the chemical to find the DNA in cells, the cells must actively take it up—in other words, the chemical must be transported to the interior of the cells. This requires work by protein machines in the cell, just like all the other work that cells do. Additionally, once they have successfully transported the chemical into their interior, cells must do more work to actively prevent the chemical from leaking out and from being destroyed before it has had an opportunity to wreck the DNA.

Because genes are switched ON and OFF in an unregulated, almost chaotic fashion in cancer cells, many different variants that manufacture different kinds of proteins have the opportunity to arise. These variants in the population of cancer cells can differ in all sorts of ways. Some may grow faster than the bulk of the cancer cells, or they may grow more slowly, or they may make different types of chemicals. They even look different under the microscope.

We have already discussed one example of this type of variation. As cancer cells change their pattern of switching genes ON and OFF, they may no longer be recognized and tolerated by the immune system as cells which belong to that individual. This particular circumstance happens to be a beneficial consequence of the instability of cancer cells. But another consequence of this instability is the emergence of a variant cell that no longer takes up an anticancer drug efficiently, or that destroys the drug much more readily, or spits it out. Even if only one such cell develops out of billions of cancer cells, that cell will now be resistant to the particular anticancer drug in use. So it will continue to grow and divide, and pretty soon it will give rise to millions of new cancer cells that are unaffected by the anticancer drug being used. Hence, sadly, it is not uncommon that following the treatment of cancer with radiation or chemicals the cancer seems to have disappeared without trace, only to reappear some time later.

Why not try another anticancer drug when this happens? Good idea, and this is often done. In fact some cancer treatments use two or even three different anticancer drugs in succession, or even at the same time. And in some cases this strategy will result in a cure when the use of a single drug did not. This switching from one type of anticancer drug to another, or the use of multiple anticancer drugs at the same time, is one of the many ways oncologists continue to refine and improve the treatment of cancer. But you must understand that it takes a long time to properly test all the possible combinations of drugs that appear on the market as potential cures for cancer, and to find out what works best. And experience shows that the same problem often happens again. In other words, yet another changed cancer cell can arise that is no longer affected by the second, or the third, chemical. Eventually some cancer cells can change in ways that make them resistant to all the many chemicals that we have at our disposal for treating cancer.

What's the future of cancer treatment?

23

The glory of medicine is that it is always moving forward. . .

—*William J. Mayo*

Of course we all continue to hope that one day a chemical will be discovered that kills or interferes with the growth of cancer cells but that has absolutely no effect on any normal cells. The world is full of chemicals and there is always the possibility that such a wonder drug may emerge, either as a natural compound or as one made in the laboratory for some other purpose. It is not very rational to blindly test hundreds of chemicals as potential anticancer agents in the hope of hitting the jackpot, particularly when that jackpot may be nonexistent. That's not what cancer research is about. So when such discoveries are made they are usually incidental to some other area of research. Let's examine a hypothetical scenario. A student may be interested in understanding how DNA is copied in cells, perhaps in bacterial cells—about as far removed from humans as one can get. One day he discovers that in a particular experiment something is seriously interfering with the copying of DNA in the bacteria. The student is panicked because he has been in graduate school for five years now and his Ph.D. thesis depends on learning how cells copy DNA. So he turns to his professor for help. Our more experienced scientist recognizes that this observation may be important and she convinces her student to find out what exactly is causing this problem with copying DNA. The student goes back to the bench and after some months he comes back to tell his professor that he has identified a chemical in the liquid that he has been using as food for the bacteria to live and grow. The chemical is isolated and when tested in cancer cells, lo and behold, it is very effective in killing them!

This kind of situation is not at all far-fetched. Recently a chemical was indeed discovered that shows very interesting promise for the treatment of certain cancers in women, especially cancer of the ovary. It is called *taxol* and comes from the bark of Pacific yew trees, of all things. This naturally occurring compound has attracted a lot of attention in the press because its use has created a thriving market for (and hence a threat to the future of) yew trees. It takes about sixty pounds of yew bark to treat one person and it has been estimated that the amount of taxol that the National Cancer Institute will require for testing purposes will cost about 38,000 trees a year! But like every other form of cancer treatment this one will have to be properly evaluated in controlled clinical trials and we'll have to wait and see just how well this early promise is fulfilled.

What exactly do we mean by a *controlled clinical trial?* The concept is one that you should understand something about, because people are often frustrated that government agencies such as the Food and Drug Administration, which regulates the marketing of all drugs, are not aggressive enough in getting promising treatments on the market. Chemicals that may prevent cancer, such as vitamin A and other anticarcinogens we talked about earlier, or, like taxol, that may be useful for treating cancer, usually surface through preliminary studies of one sort or another. Proving their effectiveness conclusively is quite another matter. It means testing the drug long enough and in a large enough number of people that the results can be clearly evaluated. In order to do this properly, it is important to evaluate an equal number of people of about the same age and with the same types of cancer who did *not* receive the treatment. If something really works, one would expect to observe good results in patients who received the treatment, but not in those who didn't.

This might seem intuitively obvious. But in fact most new drugs tested don't provide a dramatic all-or-none effect. They generally improve the outcome of the treatment *somewhat*, compared to some other treatment, and it can sometimes be difficult to be certain that the improvement is really due to the drug and not to unknown factors.

For example, let's assume that the five-year relative survival rate for a particular type of cancer was established to be 75 percent in 1980. In other words, 75 percent of people diagnosed with this type of cancer in 1975 lived for at least another five years after treatment. In 1986 a potentially promising new drug is discovered and shown to yield a five-year relative survival rate of 85 percent. But if the survival after using this chemical was never compared to the survival in people with cancer who didn't get this particular drug, we may never know whether the improved survival was due to the fact that the diagnosis of that type of cancer improved since 1985, or the fact that many people changed their diet around 1985, or some other variable.

Rest assured that scientists are not simply sitting around waiting for the chance discovery of a magic bullet for cancer cells. Many are working actively to devise new and imaginative strategies for selectively killing cancer cells based on our increasing understanding on how cancerous changes in cells actually happen. Quite obviously, the more we understand about how the process of cancer happens, the greater is the likelihood that we will be able to design anticancer treatments based on rational strategies.

Earlier we talked about the discovery of oncogenes, "cancer genes" which control the normal growth of cells, but which when altered (mutated), or made in the wrong amount or at the wrong time, can cause a cell to become uncontrolled in its growth. Cancer researchers are trying to find out precisely how the protein machines that these genes specify do this, in the hope and expectation that they will be able to find chemicals that stop them from doing whatever makes the cell grow in an uncontrolled way.

Another hot area of cancer research that shows a lot of promise for cancer treatment takes off from our understanding of the phenomenon of *immune surveillance*, which we talked about earlier; the natural ability of certain cells in the immune system to hunt down and kill cancer cells. The general term for these types of treatment is *immunotherapy*. Let me give you an example of one such immunotherapy strategy that is currently in the testing stage. Some of the white blood cells in the immune system that have a particular ability for tracking down cancer cells are lymphocytes that can burrow deep into the interior of cancers. They are called *tumor-infiltrating lymphocytes (TILs)*. But these cells don't kill cancer cells very efficiently—they are potent guns, but they are often loaded with ineffectual bullets. Scientists are now working on the idea of providing these special lymphocytes with more potent bullets. How can this be done?

As I indicated earlier, one of the wonders of this golden age of molecular biology is the ability to isolate (clone) virtually any gene from the DNA of a cell and introduce it into other cells. So here is a potential future cancer treatment scenario. We search for genes that encode the instructions for making proteins that are particularly poisonous to cells. There are lots of such proteins around in nature, which is why so many natural things are harmful. Plants have poisons; snake venom contains poisons. Cells that normally kill other cells, such as bacteria and viruses, have poisons. One particularly lethal cell poison, called ricin, comes from the seeds of the castor oil plant. (You might remember that some years ago a man was killed in the heart of London in a true-life James Bond manner by the injection of ricin loaded in the point of an umbrella.) We isolate and reproduce (clone) one or more of these "poison" genes. Now we remove the specialized lymphocytes, the TILs of the immune system that have a particular affinity for cancer cells, directly from the blood of a patient with cancer. We put the cloned "poison" gene into these cells and we reintroduce the cells into the patient's blood. Now we have loaded our potent gun with a very efficient bullet! Every time one of these TILs finds a cancer cell it should deliver a death blow to that cell, *and only to that cell,* because it doesn't latch on to normal cells.

Cancer researchers are becoming more and more innovative at exploiting the fact that cells in the immune system can selectively track down and kill cancer cells and leave normal cells undisturbed. So there are many variations of this basic theme under development. The general theme is always to make the gun bigger and more accurate and make the bullets more effective.

Will any or all of these strategies work? It's too early to tell. The good news is that these ideas for treating cancer are novel, rational, and based on new information about cancer, and the technology to implement and to refine them is growing rapidly. This is the power of science, particularly as we move into the twenty-first century. I say particularly, because the progress of science and technology is not linear. There are dry spells and there are fertile spells. You should take comfort and hope from the unassailable fact that right now we are in a particularly fertile and productive era, an era characterized by unprecedented opportunities for understanding and treating human disease. I have no doubt that the scourge of cancer will fall victim to these opportunities and that future decades, perhaps even in our lifetime, will witness what we have dreamed of for so long— the ultimate cure for cancer.

Is there a connection between cancer and one's emotional state?

24

This question was left until late in the book because its answer is certainly the most speculative. There are some cancer experts who might answer in the affirmative. Many will almost certainly answer no. My personal answer is that I don't know. I have tried to impress upon you the marvelous progress in our understanding of human biology during the past thirty five years. This is true of genes and genetics and "DNA kinds of things." But there are areas of biomedical study that remain deep dark mysteries and the human mind is definitely one of them. The entire realm of mind-body relationships is one about which we have a very limited understanding. But this area of biology is beginning to develop, and fields with impressive-sounding names like *psychoneuroimmunology* are emerging.

My own intuition as a biologist is that it is inconceivable that the mind does not influence the body and its functions. Perhaps the question really should be to what *extent* one's emotional and psychological state can influence the causation, progression, and treatment of cancer, and whether this extent is really measurable. I will simply give you the following facts: There is no good scientific evidence that mood or psychological state either predisposes one to cancer, hastens its course, or reduces the effectiveness of treatment. On the other hand, a recent follow-up of women treated for breast cancer suggested that women who participated in a breast cancer support group may have a better prognosis (better prospects for survival) than those who did not praticipate in such a group. In view of this suggestion, this particular study has recently been extended to a larger group of women.

Several other studies warrant some mention, if only to give you some awareness of how interesting—and also how controversial—the field of *psychosomatic medicine,* the study of mind-body relations, can be. You have probably heard of the type A personality, the aggressive, driven type who often has outbursts of anger and impatience, and the frequent suggestion that this personality type is more prone to heart disease than less "hotheaded" types. Several studies have suggested that cancer may be associated with a different personality type, called type C. The typical type-C personality is someone who rarely if ever shows outward signs of anger and rage but who carries a deep-seated sense of frustration and hostility. In the early 1970s a group of psychiatrists in England developed the notion of this C-type personality and its relationship to breast cancer. They carried out a study in which women with breast lumps were examined for the presence or absence of cancer. The women were also given extensive psychological tests before the results of the breast biopsies were known to the psychiatrists.

In this study the one psychological feature that correlated best with the presence or absence of cancer was "suppression of anger." Other emotional parameters such as stress or a sense of loss were equal in both groups. A different study by a group in the United States came to a very similar conclusion. They found this personality type to be particularly common in a group of patients with melanoma, the type of cancer that affects pigmented cells in the skin.

The role of the mind in the treatment of cancer is equally controversial, perhaps more so than the aspect of cancer causation. Several studies have hinted at a complicated biological connection between the brain and the immune system. The nature of this connection is still very poorly understood and it is an area of intense interest. As you will recall from our earlier discussions, we know that the immune system plays a very important role in our defenses against the growth and progression of very small cancers. Some treatment facilities have therefore integrated the notion of a "positive" state of mind into conventional cancer treatment programs. Patients are taught to visualize individual lymphocytes seeking out and destroying cancer cells in their bodies. If you are a cancer patient and you believe that in visualizing your white blood cells attacking and destroying cancer cells in your body you are helping this mission of search and destroy, I would be the last person in the world to dissuade you from that conviction. You may be correct. By the same token, however, if you do not believe this, or if you are unable to achieve such visualization, I do not believe for an instant that you are compromising your chances of being cured from cancer and neither should you.

Above and beyond all else, do not under any circumstances expose yourself to any form of treatment that is unproven with respect to cancer, but which may be harmful to your health. And do not under any circumstances forgo established and scientifically proven treatments for cancer for unproven ones. Finally, as a matter of good common sense, stay as healthy as you possibly can. Like any serious disease, cancer has a tendency to sensitize people to their bodies and to their state of health, both physically and psychologically. This is a most positive thing. Only good can emerge from taking care of yourself. Rest often, eat sensibly, exercise, and enjoy your life to the best of your ability.

Guilt is not an uncommon syndrome among people with cancer. It comes from the notion that somehow they didn't look after themselves properly and so this is their punishment—they caused their own cancer. This is one of the problems that I personally have with some of the self-help books. These books tend to talk cancer patients into believing that in the same way that they caused their cancer they can now cure their cancer. I hope this book has convinced you that cancer is not in the mind. It is caused by agents in the environment and by natural chemicals and by chemicals our cells make and by "cancer genes" not working properly. *You did not cause your cancer!*

A final message to those of you who are relatives and loved ones of people with cancer. Remember that the emotional shock of being diagnosed with cancer relates not only to the fear that we all have of this disease, but also to the fact that it often happens suddenly and unexpectedly and generally quite late in one's life. Remember that the average age for the diagnosis of all cancers in the United States and Europe, including childhood cancers, is 60 to 65. It goes without saying that your relatives and friends with cancer will need your support and your love more than ever. But support doesn't simply mean being there to share their grief and hold their hand. Support means being there to help them find the discipline and courage they need to endure difficult and sometimes debilitating treatments when they are on the verge of quitting. It means arguing for rational decisions about treatment and dissuading them from seeking irrational and unproven alternative therapies. It means helping them through the difficult phases of emotional adjustment, which initially may include periods of intense anger and denial. And it means helping them recognize and recognizing yourself that in 1992 and beyond, the diagnosis of cancer is most definitely not a sentence of death. Many thousands of people successfully conquer cancer and continue to lead productive, fulfilled, and energetic lives, often with new insights and with new and more sustaining priorities and values.

Many aspects of the role of psychological factors in cancer, both with respect to their possible role in cancer causation and in cancer cure are very well treated in a book by Henry Dreher, *Your Defense Against Cancer: The Complete Guide To Cancer Prevention*, which I have included in the section of suggestions for further reading at the end of this book.

How do I get
more information
about cancer?

25

Knowledge itself is power.
— *Francis Bacon*

This book was primarily motivated by my concern about how generally uninformed most people are about cancer as a disease entity and particularly as a biological phenomenon. In the context of a limited and simplified treatment of this massive and complex topic I have necessarily neglected many aspects of the cancer problem. In particular, while recognizing that cancer is a large group of diseases I have not attempted to address detailed but important aspects of the many different types of cancer. If you have or have had cancer I am sure that you are particularly interested in learning more about your specific type of the disease, especially its particular prognosis and the treatments most frequently used to cure it. For these details I urge you to consult the general practitioners and oncologists who have been treating you. Additionally, at the end of the book I have provided a list of some other books written primarily for the general reader on the topic of cancer. This list is by no means comprehensive, but it is representative of other more detailed and specific writings on various aspects of cancer.

In the process of engaging doctors and especially oncologists in discussions, don't be embarrassed, shy, or afraid. Believe me when I tell you that contrary to popular belief, there really is no conspiracy among doctors to keep the lay public ignorant of the discipline of medicine in the interests of maintaining some sort of mythical exalted status. I assure you that the great majority of doctors are genuinely interested in providing their patients with any information they require. Regrettably, many are simply so busy they find it very difficult to take sufficient time to establish and maintain an open dialogue with patients, and very often they fail to recognize that what is commonplace and obvious to them in the field of medicine is bewildering and confusing to those whose formal education is in another field.

Wherever possible consult with others who have already had the treatments that you are about to embark on. Their firsthand personal experience can provide a wealth of specific information that your doctor is probably not even aware of because he or she has never had chemotherapy or radiotherapy. I have a relative who has been treated for breast cancer. During her postoperative radiotherapy she encountered a myriad of small but important practical problems, both physical and psychological in nature, that were important to her as a patient, but which had obviously not occurred to the radiotherapist or his staff. After her treatment she was motivated to write a short guide stressing these practical aspects of the experience of radiotherapy from the patient's point of view. This type of help would make extremely reassuring reading for anyone who was about to embark on a course of radiotherapy for the first time. Many hospitals and clinics provide such pamphlets.

My advice is ask, ask, and ask again, until you have all the information you want. Don't be afraid to remind your physicians of their obligation to keep you well informed and don't be afraid to gently remind them of how they might wish to be treated if they were the patients instead of the doctors.

Finally, several official and more informal organizations are comprehensive repositories for a wealth of information on many aspects of cancer and will provide information on request. In particular I would recommend the American Cancer Society, a private organization that not only provides financial support for cancer research, but also publishes an extensive literature on numerous aspects of cancer, including cancer statistics of all sorts. You and your doctor might want to note that the American Cancer Society publishes and distributes free of charge a small journal every two months called *Ca-A Cancer Journal For Clinicians,* which features a series of articles on widely ranging aspects of cancer. While intended primarily for physicians, many of the articles are very informative for the general reading audience. Write to: American Cancer Society, 1599 Clifton Road, N.E., Atlanta, GA 30329, or to the American Cancer Society in your state for further information.

There are myriad organizations around the world that offer many diverse forms of assistance and information. Every group will offer a different kind of approach and you may need to search for the right group to fit your needs. Sharing your own information will have a healing effect on your emotional health and in every group there will be those who have a different technique in coping with their illness that might offer an appropriate addition to your coping skills. In any case, the cathartic effect of just being associated with or having access to others who share the same challenges of living with or surviving cancer is available through national hot lines or local chapters of national organizations. Listings of some of the many resources available both in the United States and in other parts of the world, follow. They have been organized under both a general heading and according to particular types of cancer. You would also do well to remember that every major metropolitan area telephone directory has multiple local listings, usually found under the heading "Cancer."

GENERAL CANCER HELP RESOURCES
IN THE UNITED STATES

Cancer Research Institute
133 East 58th Street
New York, NY 10022
(212) 688-7515

Cancer Care, Institute of the
  National Cancer Foundation
1180 Avenue of the Americas
New York, NY 10036
(212) 302-2400

Cancer Federation, Inc. (CFI)
21250 Box Springs Rd., #209
Moreno Valley, CA 92387
(714) 682-7989

Cancer Guidance Institute (CGI)
1323 Forbes Ave., Suite 200
Pittsburgh, PA 15219
(412) 261-2211

The Chemotherapy Foundation
183 Madison Avenue, Suite 403
New York, NY 10016
(212) 213-9292

The National Coalition for
  Cancer Survivorship
1700 Rockville Pike, # 295
Rockville, MD 20852
(301) 230-0831

The Wellness Community
22 Colorado Ave.
Santa Monica, CA 90404
(213) 453-2300

Cancer Control Society
2043 North Berendo Street
Los Angeles, CA 90027
(213) 663-7801 (messages)

I Can Cope
American Cancer Society
1599 Clifton Road, N.E.
Atlanta, GA 30329
(404) 320-3333

Cancervive, Inc.
6500 Wilshire Blvd., Suite 500
Los Angeles, CA 90048
(213) 655-3758 (messages)

American Cancer Society
Cancer Response System
1-800-ACS-2345

CanSurmount
American Cancer Society
1599 Clifton Road, N.E.
Atlanta, GA 30329
(404) 320-3333

Physician Data Query (PDQ)
A computer database of
cancer treatment information
for patients and families
as well as doctors
National Cancer Institute
Building 31, Room 10A24
9000 Rockville Pike
Bethesda, MD 20892
1-800-4-CANCER

167

CANCER ANSWERS

Life After Loss
American Cancer Society
1599 Clifton Road, N.E.
Atlanta, GA 30329
(404) 320-3333

R.A. Bloch Cancer Foundation
H and R Block Bldg.
4410 Main
Kansas City, MO 64111
(816) 932-8453

TOUCH (Today Our Under-
standing of Cancer is Hope)
Laurie Langer
(205) 879-2242

HELP RESOURCES IN THE UNITED STATES FOR PARTICULAR TYPES OF CANCER

Breast Cancer

The Susan G. Komen
  Breast Cancer Foundation
5005 LBJ Freeway, Suite 730
Dallas, TX 75224
1-800-I'M AWARE

The National Alliance of Breast
  Cancer Organizations (NABCO)
1180 Avenue of the Americas
New York, NY 10036
(212) 719-0154

ENCORE
YWCA National Board
726 Broadway
New York, NY 10003
(212) 614-2827

Reach to Recovery
American Cancer Society
19 West 56th Street
New York, NY 10019
(212) 586-8700

The Y-ME National Breast
  Cancer Organization
18220 Harwood Avenue
Homewood, IL 60430
(708) 799-8228
(800) 221-2141

Leukemia

Leukemia Society of America
733 Third Avenue
New York, NY 10017
(212) 573-8484

National Leukemia Association
585 Stewart Ave., Suite 536
Garden City, NY 11530
(516) 222-1944 (messages)

Skin Cancer

Skin Cancer Foundation
245 Fifth Avenue, Suite 2402
New York, NY 10016
(212) 725-5176

Cancer Of The Larynx

Lost Cord Club (may be called
    something else locally)
American Cancer Society
1599 Clifton Road, N.E.
Atlanta, GA 30329
(404) 320-3333

Lung Cancer

American Lung Association
1740 Broadway
New York, NY 10019
(212) 315-8700

Cancer Of The Brain

American Brain Tumor
    Association
3725 N. Talman Ave.
Chicago, IL 60618
(312) 286-5571

Childhood Cancers

Association for Research of
    Childhood Cancer
P.O. Box 251
Buffalo, NY 14225-0251
(716) 681-4433

Candlelighters Childhood
    Cancer Foundation
1312 18th St., N.W., #200
Washington, DC 20036
(202) 659-5136
(800) 366-2223

169

CANCER ANSWERS

Cancer of the Bladder, Colon, and Rectum

United Ostomy Association
36 Executive Park, Suite 120
Irvine, CA 92714
(716) 660-8624

HOTLINES

The American Cancer Society's National Toll-free Hotline: (800) ACS-2345. Information on all forms of cancer, and information on the ACS-sponsored "Reach to Recovery" program.

The Cancer Information Service, sponsored by the National Cancer Institute: (800) 422-6237.

The Y-ME National Organization for Breast Cancer Information National Toll-free Hotline: (800) 221-2141, 9:00 a.m. to 5:00 p.m., CST. (Or 24 hours at (708) 799-8228).

The Susan Komen Alliance Treatment and Information Line: (800) 462-9273.

INTERNATIONAL CANCER HELP RESOURCES

Cancer Research Campaign
2 Carlton House Terrace
London SW1Y 5AR
071-930-8972

Imperial Cancer Research Fund
P.O. Box 124, Lincoln's Inn Fields
London WC2A 3PX
071-242-0200

Colostomy Welfare Group
38-9 Eccleston Square
London SW1V 1PB
071-828-5175 (12 branches)

Leukaemia Research Fund
43 Great Ormond Street
London WC1N 3JJ
071-405-0101

Leukaemia Care Society
14 Kingfisher Court
Vennybridge, Pinhoe
Exeter EX4 8JN
0392-64848

Breast Care and Mastectomy
  Association
15-19 Britten St.
London SW3 3TZ
071-867-1103

Cancer Relief
Macmillan Fund
Anchor House
Britten Street
London SW3 3TZ
071-351-7811

Ulster Cancer Foundation
40 Eglantine Avenue
Belfast BT9 6DX
0232-663281

Women's National Cancer
  Control Campaign
128 Curtain Road
London EC2A 3AR
071-729-1735

British Association for Cancer
c/o Institute of Biology
20 Queensberry Place
London SW7 2DZ
071-581-8333

BACUP (British Association
  of Cancer United Patients)
121/123 Charterhouse St.
London EC1M 6AA
071-608-1785

British Association for
  Cancer Research
c/o Paterson Laboratories
Christie Hospital and
  Holt Radium Institute
Manchester M20 9BX

Cancer Aftercare and
  Rehabilitation Society
Lodge Cottage, Church Lane
Timsbury, Bath BA3 1LF
0761-70731

Leukaemia Society
45 Craigmoor Avenue,
  Queen's Park
Bournemouth
0202-37459

Manchester Regional Committee
  for Cancer Education
Kinnaird Road
Manchester M20 9QL
061-434-7721

Mastectomy Association of
  Great Britain
1 Colworth Road
Croydon CR0 7AD
081-654-8643
(1,500 volunteer helpers
  nationwide)

National Society for Cancer Relief
Michael Sobell House
30 Dorset Square
London NW1 6AL
071-402-8125

CANCER ANSWERS

Canadian Cancer Society
130 Bloor Street W., Suite 101
Toronto, Ontario, Canada M5S
2V7
(416) 961-7223

Women's National Cancer
  Control Campaign
1 South Audley Street
London W1Y 5DQ
071-400-7532

European Organization for
  Research on Treatment
  of Cancer (EORTC)
Institut Jules Bordet
1000 Brussels, Belgium

World Federation for Cancer Care
(Federation Mondiale
  pour les Soins du Cancer)
37 Golden Square
London W1R 4AL

WHO Melanoma Programme
Instituto Nazionale Tumori
via Veneziana 1
I-20133 Milan, Italy

SUGGESTIONS FOR FURTHER READING

The following books are representative selections of the many books on cancer intended for the general reader. My book should have provided you with a good start for understanding them. The books are paperback unless hardcover is specified.

General

Understanding Cancer. John Laszlo, Perennial Library, Harper and Row, 1988.
    A comprehensive discussion of many aspects of cancer, including diagnosis, screening and detection, the biology of cancer and cancer treatment (383 pages).

Cancer Biology: Readings from Scientific American. With Introductions by Errol C. Friedberg, W. H. Freeman, 1986.
    A series of articles mainly on the biology of cancer, reprinted from *Scientific American* and organized into sections with explanatory introductions (156 pages).

Cancer: What It Is and How It's Treated. Howard Smedley, Karol Sikora and Rob Stepney, Basil Blackwell Ltd.,1985.
A discussion of many aspects of cancer, including cancer causation, diagnosis, and treatment (180 pages).

Cancer: Science and Society. John Cairns, W. H. Freeman, 1978.
A comprehensive discussion of cancer statistics, cancer epidemiology, and aspects of the biology of cancer (199 pages).

Cancer Prevention and Early Diagnosis

Your Defense Against Cancer: The Complete Guide to Cancer Prevention. Henry Dreher, Perennial Library, Harper and Row, 1990.
Emphasizes dietary, lifestyle, and psychological factors aimed at the prevention of cancer (373 pages).

Make Sure You Do Not Have Breast Cancer. Philip Strax, St. Martin's Press, 1989.
A comprehensive discussion of breast cancer, including breast cancer screening and detection (118 pages).

Recovery from Cancer

Cancervive: The Challenge of Life After Cancer. Susan Nessim and Judith Ellis, Houghton Mifflin, 1991.
A personal discussion of cancer by the organizer of Cancervive, a national cancer support group (hardcover, 264 pages).

The Cancer Conqueror: An Incredible Journey to Wellness. Greg Anderson, Andrews and McMeel, 1990.
A personal account of a single individual's battle with cancer (153 pages).

The Race Is Run One Step at a Time: My personal Struggle—And Everywoman's Guide—To Taking Charge of Breast Cancer. Nancy Brinker with Catherine McEvily Harris, Simon and Schuster, 1990.
A detailed discussion of many aspects of breast cancer (223 pages).

CANCER ANSWERS

Triumph: Getting Back to Normal When You Have Cancer. Marion Morra
and Eve Potts, Avon Books, 1990.
  An emphasis on the process of dealing with and recovering from
cancer (297 pages).

*From Victim to Victor:The Wellness Community Guide to Fighting for Recovery
for Cancer Patients and Their Families.* Harold H. Benjamin with Richard
Trubo, Dell Publishing Co., 1987.
  A discussion of many aspects of cancer with a particular emphasis
on dealing with social and psychological reactions to cancer and being
a cancer patient (218 pages).

GLOSSARY OF TERMS

Adenoma A benign tumor of epithelial cells. Also called
  adenomatous polyp.

AIDS Acquired immune deficiency syndrome. A disease
  caused by a virus called the AIDS or HIV virus, during
  which the immune system is depressed leading to a high
  risk of getting some type of cancer.

Alternative cancer treatments Suggested "treatments" for
  cancer that have not been proven to be of any value.

Anticarcinogen A substance that helps prevent cancer.

Antimutagen A substance that helps prevent gene mutations.

Areola The pink (or brown) tissue immediately surrounding
  the nipple.

Autologous bone marrow transplantation The reintroduction
  of one's own bone marrow cells following their prior
  removal and storage.

Autopsy An after death procedure during which all organs
  and tissues are carefully examined for evidence of disease.

Basal cell carcinoma A particular type of skin cancer.

Benign neoplasm A description of any tumor that does not spread to other parts of the body.

Beta carotene A precursor of vitamin A found in dark green and yellow vegetables.

Biopsy The removal of a small piece of tissue from the body to determine whether or not it is cancerous.

Bone marrow The soft pulpy part of a bone in which various types of blood cells develop.

Cancer A disease process characterized by the uncontrolled growth of cells.

Cancer epidemiology The study of the occurrence of cancer in different parts of the world and in different populations.

Carcinogen Any substance that is known to cause cancer in humans or animals.

Carcinogenesis Any process whereby cells become cancerous.

Carcinoma A malignant tumor that arises from epithelial cells.

CAT scan Computerized axial tomography, a special technique for making and viewing images of organs in the body.

Cell division A process by which a single (parent) cell gives rise to two new (daughter) cells.

Cells The individual living units of which all organisms are composed. Cells are organized into tissues and organs.

Cervix The portion of the womb (uterus) that forms its entrance.

Chemotherapy The treatment of cancer by using chemicals that kill cancer cells.

Congenital defects Defects in any part of the body that one is born with. Also called **congenital malformations.**

Connective tissue A term used to describe the tissue that connects epithelium to the deeper tissues of the body.

Controlled clinical trial Comparison of the results of a particular treatment for cancer in patients who received the treatment with those who did not receive the treatment

DNA The substance in all cells of which genes are made.

DNA damage Alterations of the chemical units of DNA that can result in mutations in genes.

DNA repair Processes whereby damaged DNA is fixed.

Duke's classification A classification of the different stages of cancer of the colon.

Epithelial cells Cells that line surfaces in the body, such as the skin, the intestines, and the respiratory tract.

Epithelium The tissue that covers the skin and also many other surfaces in the body, such as the surface of the intestines and the surface of the air passages.

Estrogen A hormone produced mainly by the ovaries in women.

Exponential growth An increase in the number of something (such as cells), by a process of strict doubling. See also **growth.**

Fibroblasts Cells in the connective tissue of the body that can give rise to fibrosarcomas.

Fibroid A benign tumor of the wall of the uterus.

Fibrosarcoma A cancer that develops from cells called fibroblasts.

Fine needle aspiration (FNA) A special technique using a needle to remove a very tiny amount of tissue from a tumor in order to diagnose the presence and type of cancer.

Frozen section The diagnosis of cancer by removing tissue from the body, freezing it, and immediately examining it under the microscope.

Gene   A unit of DNA that specifies the manufacture of a particular protein.

Gene cloning   The isolation of individual genes from the DNA of cells.

Genetic code   A code contained in genes which determines the manufacture of proteins.

Genetic material   Genes and the DNA from which they are made.

Grading   The classification of cancers according to the appearance of the cancer cells under the microscope. Low-grade cancers often grow more slowly than high-grade cancers. See also staging.

Growth   As applied to normal cells, an increase in the number of cells in a tissue or organ of any living form.

Hematoma   A swelling caused by a bruise under the skin.

Hereditary multiple polyposis   A hereditary disease in which one is born with many benign polyps (tumors) of the intestine.

Heterologous bone marrow transplantation   The transplantation of bone marrow cells derived from a different, but biologically-related individual.

Human immunodeficiency virus (HIV)   Another name for the virus that causes AIDS.

Immune surveillance   The process whereby the immune system seeks out and kills cancer cells in the body.

Immune system   The system in the body that recognizes and kills foreign cells, including infectious bacteria.

Immunotherapy A general term for all cancer treatments that manipulate the immune system in some way.

Inoperable A description of any cancer that cannot be treated by a surgical operation.

Intestinal polyp A benign tumor of the intestine.

Invasion A process that describes the spread of cancer cells into the surrounding tissues.

Jaundice A state in which the skin and eyes are yellow because of the accumulation of excessive amounts of bile in the blood. This often happens when the bile duct is blocked.

Leiomyosarcoma A type of muscle-cell cancer.

Leukemia A malignant tumor that arises from white cells in the blood called leukocytes.

Leukocytes See **white blood cells.**

Lipoma A benign tumor that arises from fat cells.

Lumpectomy A surgical procedure for the treatment of breast cancer in which just the cancer lump itself and some surrounding tissue is removed.

Lymph A special fluid made by cells, which circulates in the lymphatic vessels of the body.

Lymph nodes Small round structures located at frequent intervals in the lymphatic system. Lymph is filtered as it passes through the lymph nodes. Also called **lymph glands.**

Lymphatic system A system composed of vessels similar to blood vessels, through which a fluid called lymph circulates.

Lymphocytes Cells that are members of the family of white blood cells (leukocytes). They are also found in **lymph nodes.**

Lymphoma A malignant tumor that arises from lymphocytes.

Magnetic resonance imaging (MRI) A special technique for viewing organs and tissues of the body.

Malignant Description of any tumor that has the ability to spread to different parts of the body. The terms "malignant tumor" and "cancer" are the same.

Mammogram A special X-ray technique for detecting small lumps in the breast.

Mastectomy A surgical treatment for cancer in which part or all of the breast is removed. See also **radical mastectomy.**

Melanin A brown pigment made by certain cells in the skin which gives different people different skin colors.

Melanoma A cancer which develops from cells in the skin that carry melanin pigment.

Metastasis The spread of an original cancer to different parts of the body.

Molecular biology The study of cells at the molecular level, including the isolation and manipulation of genes and proteins.

Mutagen Any substance that can cause mutation or alteration in the structure of a gene. Also called **mutagenic agent.**

Mutagenesis Any process whereby mutations arise in the genes of cells.

Mutation An alteration in the structure of a gene.

Neoplasm Another term for both malignant and nonmalignant tumors.

Occupational cancer The types of cancer that develop because of occupational exposure to carcinogens. Also called **occupational carcinogenosis.**

Oncogenes "Cancer genes." When altered in their function, such genes facilitate the development of cancerous changes in cells.

Oncologist A physician who specializes in cancer.

Oncology The medical specialty of cancer.

Osteosarcoma A malignant tumor that arises from bone cells.

Pap smear A procedure by which cells from the cervix of the uterus are placed on a glass slide and microscopically examined for cancerous change.

Papillomavirus A type of virus that has been implicated in causing cancer of the cervix.

Pathologist A physician who is specially trained to diagnose diseases by examining organs, and cells under the microscope.

Platelets Cells that are made in the bone marrow and that circulate in the blood. Platelets are required for normal blood clotting.

Polyp A benign tumor of the epithelium that is separated from the epithelial surface by a stalk.

Premalignant change A change in the appearance of cells that sometimes precedes the development of cancer in them.

Proctoscope A special instrument which can be inserted in the rectum in order to examine the intestines.

Prostate gland A small gland located near the base of the bladder in men.

Prostate specific antigen A substance produced by the prostate gland which can be helpful for the early diagnosis of prostatic cancer.

Protein A substance found in all cells. Different proteins are used to drive different types of events in cells. The manufacture of each protein is specified by a different gene.

Psychoneuroimmunology A discipline that attempts to study the interrelationships between the mind, the nervous system, and the immune system.

Psychosomatic medicine The general study of the relationship between the mind and the body.

Radiation oncology A discipline that deals with the treatment of cancer by the use of radiation, such as X-rays. Also referred to as **radiotherapy** or **radiation therapy.**

Radical mastectomy A surgical treatment for breast cancer in which the entire breast plus surrounding tissues are removed.

Red blood cells Cells in the blood which mature from precursor cells in the bone marrow and which carry oxygen to all parts of the body.

Rejection The process whereby a transplanted tissue or an organ is discarded by the immune system of the body.

Relative survival rate The survival level in a population. With regard to a particular type of cancer, the rate is adjusted to measure only those deaths that occurred from the cancer and not from other causes that might be expected in that population.

Remission A state during which a cancer appears to be disappearing or is no longer detectable by any available tests.

Retinoblastoma A malignant tumor of the retina.

Retinoids A class of substances that are similar to retinol, the form of vitamin A that occurs in foods.

Rhabdomyosarcoma A type of muscle-cell cancer.

Sarcoma A malignant tumor that arises from cells in the

supporting systems of the body, such as bone, cartilage, muscle, ligaments, and tendons.

Staging A numerical description of the extent of spread of a lymphoma in the body, with low numbers indicating earlier stages.

Statistical probability The mathematically determined likelihood that some event (such as survival from cancer) will occur.

Syndrome A collection of symptoms and signs that go together; another word for a disease entity.

Tamoxifen A compound used to treat breast cancer by interfering with the ability of estrogen to get into breast cancer cells.

Taxol A substance obtained from the bark of Pacific yew trees which appears to be useful in the treatment of cancer, especially cancer of the ovary.

Tissues Collections of the cells in one part of the body, for example, brain tissue. Different organs can be composed of one or of multiple different tissues.

Total mastectomy A surgical operation for the treatment of breast cancer in which the entire breast is removed.

Transplant The introduction of tissue (including bone marrow) or organs from one person into another.

Tumor A term often used for cancer. But the term really means "swelling" and can be used for any lump or swelling.

Tumor infiltrating lymphocytes (TILs) Cells (lymphocytes) in the immune system which have a special ability to find their way inside cancers.

Tumor progression The many steps a malignant tumor goes through from its very beginning to the time that it becomes well established in the body.

Tumor promotors   Agents which by themselves do not cause cancer, but which can facilitate and accelerate cancerous changes in cells caused by true carcinogens.

Ultrasound   A special technique using sound waves for generating images of organs in the body.

Uterus   The womb.

White blood cells   Cells in the blood which are made by special cells in the bone marrow. White blood cells are part of the immune system.

Xeroderma pigmentosum (XP)   A hereditary human disease in which people are born with an inability to repair damaged DNA.

Index

Acquired immunodeficiency
    syndrome (AIDS), 82–83,
    89–90
Adenoma, 33
Age, cancer risk and, 50–51
Alcohol, 108
Alternative cancer treatments,
    134–137, 160
American Cancer Society,
    165–166
American Joint Committee on
    Cancer Staging, 78
Amygdalin, 136
Anger, suppression of, 159
Angiosarcoma, 36
Anticarcinogens, 105–107
Antimutagens, 105
Areola, 13
Aspiration, fine needle, 40
Autologous bone marrow
    transplantation, 117
Autopsy, 75

Benign tumors, 23, 26
    malignant change in, 28–29
Beta-carotene, 107
Biopsy, 39–41

Bladder cancer
    frequency of, 46
    help resources for, 170
    survival rates for, 141
    symptoms of, 15
Bone cancer, 35, 36
Bone marrow
    cancer of. *See* Leukemia
    effect of treatment on, 115
    transplantation of, 117–119
    rejection in, 88
Brain cancer, help resources for,
    169
Breast cancer
    death rates for, 48
    diagnosis of, 39
    emotional factors in, 159
    estrogen and, 119
    frequency of, 46
    help resources for, 168, 170, 171
    metastasis in, 19
    risk of, 44–45
    staging of, 78
    survival rates for, 141, 144–145
    symptoms of, 13
    tamoxifen for, 119
    treatment of, 130

Ca—A Cancer Journal for Clinicians, 166
Cancer. *See also specific types of cancer*
  causes of. *See* Carcinogens
  cell types of, 32–36
  death rates for, 45–48
  definition of, 2, 68
  diagnosis of, 38–41
  emotional factors in, 158–161
  epidemiology of, 53
  genetic predisposition to, 94–98
  grading of, 77–78
  incidence of, 44–45, 57–58
  information sources for, 164–174
  inoperable, 112–113
  most common types of, 46–48
  natural defenses against, 86–91
  risk of, 44–45, 53–58, 69–70, 94–98. *See also* Risk factors
  reduction of, 100–109
  spread of, 17–19
  staging of, 41, 78–80
  survival in, 140–145
  symptoms of, 12–20
  treatment of. *See* Treatment
  tumors and, 22–24
Cancer cells
  defective protein and, 61, 68
  DNA damage in, 114
  drug resistance in, 148–150
  growth of, 6, 8–10, 74–80
  immune surveillance of, 88–89, 155
  instability of, 149–150
  invasion by, 9, 10
  origin of, 60–64
  treatment effects on, 113–114
  types of, 34–36
Cancer centers, 123–128

Cancer clusters, 101
Cancer epidemiology, 53
Cancer genes, 94–98
Cancer patients
  help resources for, 164–174
  personality traits of, 158–161
  support for, 161
Carcinogens
  cellular, 56–57, 70
  chemical, 51–56
    identification of, 102–103
  in cigarettes, 51–52
  definition of, 51
  DNA damage by, 67–72
  environmental, 51–58
  occupational, 53, 100
  in vegetables, 55–56
Carcinoma, 33
CAT scan, 38
Cell(s)
  cancer. *See* Cancer cells
  cancerous transformation in, 60–64
  definition of, 2
  epithelial, 33
    cancer of, 33
  growth of
    controlled, 3–6
    uncontrolled, 6, 8–10
  premalignant changes in, 83
  protein manufacture in, 61–62
  structure and function of, 60–64
  toxic byproducts of, 56–57, 70
  treatment effects on, 115–116
Cell division, 3, 66
Cervical cancer
  diagnosis of, 76, 83
  growth rate of, 76–77

survival rates for, 141
symptoms of, 14
Chemicals
cancer-causing, 51–56
identification of, 102–103
tumor-promoting, 107–109
Chemotherapy, 114
centers for, 123–128
combination, 150
controlled clinical trials for, 153–154
decisions about, 122–131
drugs used in, 116
future directions in, 152–156
resistance to, 148–150
side effects of, 115–116
Children
cancer deaths among, 45
help resources for, 169
survival rates for, 143
Chimney sweeps, scrotal cancer in, 52–53
Chondrosarcoma, 36
Cigarette smoking, 51–52, 68–70
Clinical trials, 153–154
Cloning, gene, 97–98, 155–156
Colon cancer
death rates for, 48
frequency of, 46
help resources for, 170
hereditary multiple polyposis and, 96
staging of, 72–79
survival rates for, 141, 145
symptoms of, 13
types of, 36
Colon polyps, 28, 96
Common cancer types, 46–48

Comprehensive cancer centers, 123–128
Computerized axial tomography, 38
Congenital defects, 6
Connective tissue, 35
cancer of, 34–36
Controlled clinical trials, 153–154
Cure rates, 140–145

Death rates, 45–48
Diagnosis, 38–41
biopsy in, 39–41
mammography in, 39
Diet, 104–109
DNA, 63–64
cell division and, 66–67
structure of, 71–72
DNA damage, 67, 86–87
in cancer cells, 114
environmental causes of, 67–70
natural causes of, 70–71
DNA repair, 69–70, 86–91
Doctors, communication with, 164–165
Drugs, chemotherapeutic, 116. *See also* Chemotherapy
Dukes classification, for colon cancer, 78–79

Elderly, cancer risk in, 50–51
Emotional factors, 158–161
Endocrine therapy, 119
Environmental causes of cancer, 51–58
Epidemiology, 53
Epithelial cells, 33
Epithelium, 33
Estrogen, in breast cancer, 119

Evolution, 58
Experimental treatments, 134–137
Exponential growth, 4, 5

Fibroblast, 35
Fibroid tumors, 26
Fibrosarcoma, 36
Fine needle aspiration, 40
Foods
    anticarcinogens in, 55–56, 105–
        107
    carcinogens in, 55–56
Frozen section, 41

Gene(s), 63
    cancer, 94–98
Gene cloning, 97–98, 155–156
Genetic code, 71–72
Genetic material, 66
Genetic mutations, 67–72, 103
    defenses against, 86–91
    increased cancer risk and, 94–98
Geographic variations, in cancer
        incidence, 47–48, 101–102
Grading, 77–78
Growth
    cellular
        controlled, 3–6
        uncontrolled, 6, 8–10
    exponential, 4, 5
Guilt, 160–161

Help resources, 164–174
Hematoma, 22
Hereditary multiple polyposis, 96
Heterologous bone marrow
        transplantation, 117
Hormone therapy, 119

Hotlines, 170
Human immunodeficiency virus
        (HIV), 82–83

Immune surveillance, 88–89, 155
Immune system, 88
Immunotherapy, 155
Information sources, 164–174
Inoperable cancer, 112–113
Intestinal polyps, 28, 96
Invasion, by cancer cells, 9, 10

Japan, prostate cancer in, 101–102
Jaundice, 14
Job-related cancers, 53, 100

Laetrile, 136
Laryngeal cancer, help resources
        for, 169
Leiomyosarcoma, 36
Leukemia, 33–34
    death rates for, 48
    frequency of, 46
    help resources for, 168, 171
    survival rates for, 141
    symptoms of, in adults, 15
Leukocytes. See White blood cells
Lifestyle factors, 101–109
Lipoma, 26
Liposarcoma, 36
Lumpectomy, 130
Lung cancer
    death rates for, 48
    frequency of, 46
    help resources for, 169
    smoking and, 51–52, 68–70
    survival rates for, 141, 144
    symptoms of, 13–14

Lymph, 18
Lymph nodes, metastasis to, 18–19
Lymphatic system, 18
Lymphocytes, 34
    tumor-infiltrating, 155
Lymphoma, 34
    frequency of, 46
    staging of, 41
    symptoms of, 15

Magnetic resonance imaging
    (MRI), 38
Malignant tumors, 23, 26
Mammography, 39
Mastectomy, 130
Melanin, 29
Melanoma, 29
    frequency of, 46
    survival rates for, 141
    symptoms of, 15
Metastasis, 17–19
Molecular biology, 72
Moles, malignant changes in, 15, 29
Mortality rates, 45–48
Mouth cancer, frequency of, 46
MRI, 38
Muscle, cancer of, 35, 36
Mutations, 67–72, 103
    defenses against, 86–91
    increased cancer risk and, 94–98

Natural defenses, against cancer,
    86–91
Natural selection, 58
Neoplasms, 22–24

Occupational carcinogenesis, 53, 100
Oncogenes, 94–98

Oncologist, 23–24
    communication with, 164–165
Oncology, 97
Oral cancer, frequency of, 46
Organ transplant, rejection of, 88
Osteosarcoma, 35, 36
Ovarian cancer, frequency of, 46

Pancreatic cancer
    frequency of, 46
    symptoms of, 14
Pap smear, 76, 83
Papillomavirus, 83
Pathologist, 40
Personality factors, 158–161
Pesticides, 55–56
Platelets, 114
Polyps, intestinal, 28, 96
Premalignant change, 83
Proctoscope, 28
Prostate cancer
    death rates for, 48
    diagnosis of, 39
    grading of, 78
    growth rate of, 75–76
    incidence of, 46, 75–76, 101–102
    staging of, 79–80
    survival rates for, 141
Prostate specific antigen (PSA), 39
Protein
    cellular manufacture of, 61–62
    defects in, 61, 68
Psychologic factors, 158–161
Psychoneuroimmunology, 158
Psychosomatic medicine, 159

Radiation, DNA damage from, 87
Radiation oncology, 128

Radiation therapy, 114
  centers for, 123–128
  decisions about, 122–131
  future directions in, 152–156
  side effects of, 115–116
Radical mastectomy, 130
Rectal cancer
  death rates for, 48
  frequency of, 46
  help resources for, 170
  survival rates for, 141
  symptoms of, 13
Red blood cells, 114
Rejection, in transplants, 88
Relative survival rates, 141–142
Remission, 140
Research, future directions in,
  152–156
Resources, for cancer patients,
  164–174
Retinoblastoma, 95–96
Retinoids, 107
Rhabdomyosarcoma, 35, 36
Risk, of getting cancer, 44–45,
  53–58, 69–70, 94–98
  reduction of, 100–109
Risk factors, 69–70
  dietary, 104–109
  environmental, 51–56
  genetic, 94–98
  lifestyle, 101–109
  occupational, 53, 100
  physiological, 98
  reduction of, 100–109

Sarcoma, 34–36
Scrotal cancer, in chimney sweeps,
  53

Skin cancer. *See also* Melanoma
  in Australia, 102
  help resources for, 169, 172
  in xeroderma pigmentosum, 90
Smoking, 51–52, 68–70
Staging, 41, 78–79
Statistical probability, 144
Stomach cancer
  frequency of, 46
  symptoms of, 14
Sunlight, DNA damage from, 86–87
Support groups, 166–172
Surgery, 112–113
  for breast cancer, 130
  centers for, 123–128
  decisions about, 122–131
Surgical biopsy, 40–41
Survival rates, 140–145
Symptoms
  early, 12–20
  general, 12–13

Tamoxifen, 119
Taxol, 153
Testicular cancer
  survival rates for, 141
  symptoms of, 16
Tissue, 4
Total mastectomy, 130
Transplant
  bone marrow, 117–119
  rejection of, 88
Treatment
  alternative, 134–137, 160
  bone marrow transplant, 117–119
  controlled clinical trials for,
    153–154
  decisions about, 122–131

drug, 114, 115–116
emotional factors in, 159–160
failure of, 148–150
future directions in, 152–156
gene, 97–98, 155–156
hormonal, 119
immunologic, 155
physical effects of, 112–120
radiation, 114, 115–116, 128
success rates for, 140–145
surgical, 112–113
Treatment centers, 123–128
Tumor, 22–24
benign, 23, 26
malignant changes in, 28–29
malignant, 23, 26
Tumor-infiltrating lymphocytes, 155
Tumor progression, 75
Tumor promoters, 107–109
Type C personality, 158–161

Ultrasound, 38–39

Ultraviolet radiation, DNA damage from, 86–87
Union Internationale Contre Cancer staging system, 78
Uterine cancer
frequency of, 46
survival rates for, 141
symptoms of, 14
Uterine fibroid tumors, 26

Vegetables
anticarcinogens in, 107
carcinogens in, 55–56
Viruses, 82–83
Vitamin A, 107
Vitamin C, 106

White blood cells, 114
cancer of. *See* Leukemia; Lymphoma
tumor-infiltrating, 155

Xeroderma pigmentosum (XP), 90